Twin Cities
UNCOVERED

The Arthurs

Seaside Press

Library of Congress Cataloging-in-Publication Data

Arthur, Lindsay G., 1917-
    Twin Cities uncovered / The Arthur Family : [written by] Lindsay G. Arthur
and Jean Arthur.
      p. cm.
    Includes Index
    ISBN 1-55622-388-9
    1. Minneapolis (Minn.)--Description and travel.   2. Saint Paul (Minn.)--
Description and travel.   I. Arthur, Jean.   II. Title.
    F614.M6A77   1995
    917.76'5790453--dc20   94-48650
                                                        CIP

Seaside Press is an imprint of Wordware Publishing, Inc.

No part of this book may be reproduced in any form or by
any means without permission in writing from
Wordware Publishing, Inc.

Printed in the United States of America

ISBN1-55622-388-9
10 9 8 7 6 5 4 3 2 1
9512

All inquiries for volume purchases of this book should be addressed to
Wordware Publishing, Inc., at 1506 Capital Avenue, Plano, Texas 75074.
Telephone inquiries may be made by calling:

(214) 423-0090

Contents

Contents

Chapter 7
Outdoor Activities

Chapter 8
Stages and Theaters

Contents

Preface

Most readers will know some of the people and places and data set forth here. Some readers will know many of them, maybe most of them. Hopefully no one will know them all. Maybe there will be some new fact, some new anecdote or rumor or legend that will titillate and maybe evoke a smile or pique the reader's curiosity.

Most everyone will find corrections; some will be right. To have checked out every fact and every statement would have been a task of years, and then the earlier information might have changed. This tome is not intended for professional researchers and does not meet their standards of accuracy. It is intended to show the wonders of our community. Its goal is to pull people off of their couches and out of their chairs to go out and see and sample the full life in this the best of all communities.

This book is intended to entice readers to visit places of interest, places of fun, places of yesterday, and places of tomorrow. Some of the places are awesome, in the preadolescent meaning of the word. Many are inspirational. A lot of them will bring smiles. Some of them may send you out to find out more. All of them are interesting.

There are no doubt places and people missed; this is a large community. Whole categories, such a restaurants, are omitted because of their transient nature or because there are so many of quality that, like churches, to mention one would require in fairness mentioning all. Even a bibliography is omitted; there are so many books about the area, some with overwhelming photography. Libraries will gladly make these available.

Most importantly, this is a book to be enjoyed more than studied, to bring home to readers that this is in fact about the best place in the whole world in which to live.

The Father of Waters

The Mississippi was known to the Ojibwa who had lived near it for a millenium as *mis-sipi*, or "Great River." And great it is! It is truly the "Father of Waters."

It defines the Twin Cities. For most of their beginning it was their umbilical cord, bringing in their needs and supplies, taking out their grain and their furs and their lumber, supplying their water and the power for sawing their seemingly endless timber and grinding their grain, supplying magnificent views of flowing waters, and giving the inspiration of a roaring falls.

It begins in Itasca, which is a Latin, not an Indian, name. Henry Schoolcraft, the Indian Commissioner in 1832, first proved that he had found the river's true head at Itasca, in Latin *veritas caput* (*verITAS CAput*). There is a large and beautiful park there now with a place where you can walk across the Mississippi River in one step. Then it flows south 2,348 miles to New Orleans, gaining strength from the Ohio and the Missouri and dozens of other tributaries to become the world's mightiest river.

Seventy-two miles of the river as it flows through the Twin Cities is recognized as a National Waterway. Minneapolis is a coined name from the Ojibwa *minne* for water and the Greek *polis* for city. Saint Paul was originally named "Pigs Eye" for Pierre Parrant, a booming, colorful, one-eyed French fur trader who opened the first saloon on the Upper Mississippi. It became so popular that you could address a letter to someone at "Pigs Eye" and it got there. Some years later, Father Galtier persuaded the powers that were that "Saint Paul" would be more dignified. In gratitude, St. Paul city leaders named a plaza after the good father. A downriver island used for a sewage plant was named for Pigs Eye, as was a beer which has become a national favorite.

The National Waterway section begins at Dayton, a town that until about two generations ago preserved much of its French language and way of life. The section ends at Hastings*, a city spread along the narrow edge of the river with so little room for the western end of a bridge over the river that the approach ramp was a high spiral. The bridge has since been replaced by a less colorful span. In the seventy-two miles of its passage, it picks up the waters of the Crow River at Dayton, the Rum River at Anoka, the Minnesota River at Fort Snelling, and the St. Croix River at Hastings, plus numerous creeks.

In between there are about 2.5 million people in the "Twin Cities." They're not really twins. St. Paul is older, more settled, Irish and Italian, predominantly Catholic. Minneapolis boasts of its newness, its aggressiveness; it is Scandinavian, German, Polish, predominantly Protestant. The two cities have been competitors since they began, but now, when they are outnumbered by their suburbs, they are working more closely together.

Near the northwestern corner of the metropolitan area, at Coon Rapids, up by Anoka*, a dam was built to generate electrical power. The dam covered up the rapids and backed up the river almost to the Crow, making it like a long lake.

Cities are built beside rivers and streams. Big cities are built beside large rivers. Some big cities are built beside large rivers with interesting islands. Minneapolis has a big river; the river has islands: Boom Island and Nicollet Island. But Minneapolis also has falls, large falls, the only major city in the world so beautifully and usefully sited. Yet for at least a century, the downtown of Minneapolis turned its

---

*   See Index or Contents for separate article on this topic.

back on its river. St. Paul did it better, it has always faced the river. And now St. Paul is doing it even better: in September 1994, the St. Paul Chamber Orchestra played a concert on a barge moored in the river to an audience of over 8,000 sitting on the grass on Navy Island. Not only did they attract a much larger audience than expected, they did it playing only the classics: Handel, Beethoven, Rossini, and Mozart.

For a century or so, in the center of Minneapolis at water level there were railroad tracks and switching yards, coal dumps, and a lot of weeds and brush. Railroad depots, grain elevators, and warehouses dominated the bluffs—all the ingredients of the industry that built the city. You could see the river from a bridge as you crossed, but that was about the only place it could be seen. All that has changed. It is now called the "Mississippi Mile."

"The Great River Road" has been built on the west side at water level with many turnouts, picnic spots, observation points, a bicycle path, pedestrian paths, pleasant street lights, with grass and trees. Eventually the segments of the road will be connected all the way to New Orleans.

Upstream on the east side, Boom Island has been converted into a nice park with a recreation area, picnic tables, promenades, and places to walk right down along the river. The long pool of water backed up from the St. Anthony dam allows private boat launching and docks for the stern-wheelers that ply the river with passengers.

Nicollet Island is almost bucolic on the upstream end, with trees and wild grass along the water and ancient multiple housing, the Eastman Flats, built along the avenue in the eighties. Many have since been demolished, but some have been restored and are in use. A short but pleasant walk is around the upstream end of the island. The center of the island is occupied by De La Salle Catholic High School with its long traditions. The south end, which used to be heavily industrialized, has converted a limestone block sash and door factory into an interesting hotel and restaurant, the Nicollet Inn, with a little park at water's edge.

The island is bisected by the Hennepin Avenue Bridge, the third bridge at the site. The first, in 1855, was a dramatic suspension bridge with tall wooden towers. The second was a simple, efficient, and unattractive steel truss. The third, finished recently, is a handsome steel tower suspension bridge designed to be reminiscent of the first.

On the west side opposite Nicollet Island, there was a skid row of twenty blocks or so which started as "Bridge Square," then, to point out the city which had grown to the south, "The Gateway." It became a gathering place for men looking for jobs in the mines and forests and railroads and farms of Minnesota. As the need for such labor decreased, it became an area for retired men to live in, with inexpensive hotels and rooming houses that had lost what glamour they had ever had. It became a distinct colony of about two thousand men and almost no women. The men were mostly on pensions and were widowers or bachelors. A careful social study found that they all idealized women, so much so that a woman was totally safe at night even from outsiders; the old men were watchful and protective. They spent their days in cafes with a newspaper or a checkerboard.

It has all been replaced with new office buildings, a new public library, several high-rise condominiums, the delightful Whitney Hotel converted from an early, granite grain building, a water fountain and reflecting pool, and parks. A new Federal Reserve building is replacing older commercial buildings along the river and the former handsome, colonnaded Union Depot. The other depot, the Milwaukee Depot, less attractive and farther from the river, is being preserved.

The former "Fed," located a few blocks away on Nicollet between Washington and Third Street, is built like a suspension bridge, constructed of two towers with suspension cables supporting the roof and floors. It allows totally pillar-less floor areas for full flexibility. The exterior has a sloping plaza and a glass facing emphasizing the suspension cables. Though of recent construction, it became untenantable because of the asbestos used.

On the east bank adjacent to Nicollet Island is an entertainment district known as "Mississippi Live," with various bars, sidewalk cafes, live shows, a movie house, gift shops, and boutiques. Main Street is down at the river's edge on the east side, a cobblestone street, park-like on the river side and used by joggers and pedestrians. Mills and elevators and factories have been preserved as they were a century ago.

The "Mississippi Mile" extends down along Main Street to a row of shops and charming restaurants and coffee houses at water's edge, and to The Museum of Questionable Medical Devices*. There are also luxury condominiums and rental apartments, with views of the river and St. Anthony Falls and the towers and skyline of the city.

Central Avenue, which includes an area of several blocks on the east side between the Hennepin Bridge and the Third Avenue Bridge, has retained and restored much of its old flavor when it was the beginning of the city. There are numerous stores and shops and restaurants. The new highrises have managed to blend in rather well.

On the edge of the Central Avenue area is Our Lady of Lourdes Roman Catholic Church, built in 1857 for the Universalist Church and converted in 1877 for a Catholic parish which added a bell tower, a transept, and a sacristy. It is well preserved, a dominating architectural presence, and very

---

*   See Index or Contents for separate article on this topic.

much a functioning church. The parish's strong French influence has been preserved. Outdoors, by the front entry, is a plaque that reads:

> *In commemoration of the courageous French explorers whose discoveries inspired French settlement and anticipated the growth of the City of Minneapolis.*

Behind Lourdes in its own little park is the Ard Godfrey House*, restored and maintained by the Women's Club of Minneapolis.

The Third Avenue Bridge, which connects Third Avenue on the west side with Central Avenue on the east side, is a gentle "S" curve crossing over the St. Anthony Falls Dam. It is a pleasant place to stroll and watch the river, to contemplate the massive amount of water pouring over the irregularly shaped dams underneath, to see boats and barges being locked through, or just to relax.

On the east side, upstream from the Third Avenue Bridge and connected to Nicollet Island by a pedestrian bridge from a railroad trestle, is Father Hennepin Park. From this point, in 1680, Father Hennepin was the first white man to see the falls, which he named after St. Anthony, his patron saint. Until the dam was built, the falls had been receding very slowly upstream as its soft limestone underpinnings eroded.

Father Hennepin was a Belgian missionary sent out in 1675 by King Louis XIV of France. He was stationed on the St. Lawrence River for about five years and then trekked west, at one time being held captive by the Indians for three months. He joined LaSalle's expedition up the Mississippi, which enabled him to see the falls.

---

*   See Index or Contents for separate article on this topic.

The Falls of Saint Anthony were known by the Dakotas as *Minnerara,* curling water, or *Owah Menah*, falling water. The area was considered sacred. Indians passing by would stop and pray and often leave an offering. It was also used as a rallying ground for a war party starting off on a sortie. It is the only falls on the entire Mississippi River—seventy-two feet high, tamed now by dams and locks, but hypnotic to look at. The dams still mill some of the flour that gave the city its start and its nickname of "Mill City," when it was the largest milling center in the United States. The dams generate some electricity, and they provide a research facility for the University of Minnesota. Mainly though they keep the limestone falls from eroding farther upstream.

There is a legend that an Indian woman, Ampata Sapa, sorrowing because her husband had married another woman, intentionally went over the falls with her children, and that her spirit still lingers in the mists.

At the downstream end of the Mississippi Mile is the Stone Arch Bridge, built by James J. Hill for his railroad but with his specific direction to make it as charming as its setting. He succeeded. It is of limestone blocks with graceful arches and curves as it crosses above the falls. It has now been converted for use by pedestrians and bicyclists who are treated to magnificent views of the river.

There is a gorge then, the river flowing its stately way through high banks with roads and trails on the tops and little boys down at the water's edge. After a rain, there are various little falls that dot the banks with their streaks of silver. Farther downstream, past Lake Street and Fiftieth Street, is another dam where there was a rapids, built by the Ford Motor Company seventy-five or so years ago for electricity for its assembly plant up on the east side.

The Minnesota Soldiers Home is perched on the west bank, as it has been since after the Spanish-American War, one of the few state-maintained homes where old soldiers can quietly fade away.

Just below the Ford Dam, Minnehaha* Creek flows in, bringing water from Lake Minnetonka*. Up the valley a ways is Minnehaha Falls, forty feet high, in a beautiful park setting, memorialized by Longfellow in the "Song of Hiawatha." At the head of the falls is a bronze statue of Hiawatha carrying Minnehaha across the stream.

Farther downstream, the Minnesota River comes from far out in the west, at the Dakota border, a principal trade route for the Indians and later for the settlers. It was originally named the St. Peter River. About sixty miles upstream from Fort Snelling is the city of St. Peter, which was one of the four largest cities in the state and vied vigorously with the other three, Stillwater, St. Paul, and Minneapolis, to be the capital of the state. Legend says that the Legislature designated St. Peter, which had developed a sizable political action fund for the purpose, but the Speaker of the House, favoring St. Paul, put the original of the bill, the only one attested by the House and the Senate, in his pocket and went fishing. The Legislature reached its compulsory adjournment date and had to go home. Unable to sign the original, the governor signed a copy, but the Supreme Court held that his signature was invalid because there was no proof that the copy was an exact duplicate of the original; every copy was necessarily a handwritten copy since no typewriters, carbon paper, or copying machines were available. Subsequently, a compromise was reached to place the capital in St. Paul, the largest city; the university in Minneapolis, the second largest; the state prison in Stillwater, the third largest; and the state hospital in St. Peter.

---

*   See Index or Contents for separate article on this topic.

Where the Minnesota joins the Mississippi, there are high bluffs, an ideal site for Fort Snelling* to control both rivers and to keep peace in the territory. In the river there is an island named "Pike" for Zebulon Pike, the man who first negotiated with the Indians for the land on which the fort was built. Colorado's towering Pike's Peak was also named for him. The fort is still very much in service, serving as an induction base for thousands of soldiers in both World Wars. It has a full reconstruction to show how life was in 1843 when Colonel Snelling took command and changed its name. In the summer, people dressed as in 1843 are glad to converse with you, but their frame of reference is 1843. As though suspended in time, they know nothing of anything that may have happened since then.

Below the fort there is a small park on the east side for picnickers and swimmers. Then the river starts its swing to the east, past Hidden Falls, to St. Paul with its high banks and commercial towers on one side and a low flood plane on the other, with an airport and factories, and residences. There is ever-growing use of the river: Navy Island where a symphony orchestra has played to a full crowd and Harriet Island where a rock concert has done the same. Beyond the commercial towers, the banks slope down to water's edge, with a cave where Pigs Eye Parrant* opened his tavern. The river sweeps to the south again, past the South St. Paul livestock yards and packing plants, until recently the biggest in the world—bigger even than Chicago's "Meat butcher to the world." The yards are now in decline as trucks and freeways make transportation possible for numerous local packers. Then the magnificent river heads south again for Hastings* and Red Wing with its potteries and then to St. Louis and New Orleans.

---

*   See Index or Contents for separate article on this topic.

More and more, all along its banks, people are turning again to the river. There are more parks. There are more high-rises. There are more boats. There are more barges taking Wyoming's coal and the Upper Midwest's grain to Chicago and Pittsburgh, St. Louis, Memphis, and New Orleans and bringing back the products of the world. The Twin Cities are finally recognizing the treasure that made it all possible from the beginning. They are asserting themselves once more as the headwaters of the Father of Waters.

A Brief History of Two Young Cities

8000 BC The Paleo-Indians moved into the vacant region from the south and settled. They lived by hunting mammoths and disappeared when the mammoths became extinct.

7000 BC Other Indians came in and settled, living on berries and small animals. They left numerous petroglyphic carvings but disappeared by 500 AD.

500 Dakota and Ojibwa moved into the land, again vacant. The number is uncertain but there were probably several thousand of them when the Europeans first appeared.

1659 Pierre Radisson and French fur traders came south into the region from Lake Superior, finding two Indian tribes: the Dakotas, often called the Sioux, meaning "snake," who lived in the open south and west; and the Ojibwa, also called the Chippewa of the Algonkian family, who lived in the heavy forests in the north. The two tribes were in almost constant warfare.

1679 The Sieur du Lhut, for whom Duluth was named, also came south from Lake Superior as far as Lake Mille Lacs, a very large lake in the center of Minnesota. He made formal claim to the land for France, a claim of which the Indians were probably not aware.

1680 Father Hennepin, who had come up the Mississippi with LaSalle, was sent on with a party farther up the river and became the first European to see St. Anthony Falls, the future location of Minneapolis, naming the magnificent falls for his patron saint and later writing the first description of the country. French exploration then ceased because of the death of Frontenac, governor of French-America, and the expenses of the War of Spanish Succession. A county was named for him.

1700   Pierre Le Sueur ascended the Minnesota River past the area later named Lesueur County to the Blue Earth River where Mankato was later sited.

1762   France ceded all its lands west of the Mississippi to Spain. The Indians of course were not consulted and hadn't known that it was not their land.

1763   As a result of the Seven Years War, France ceded all of its lands east of the Mississippi to England. According to the Europeans, what later became St. Paul thus moved from French to English possession, and what later became Minneapolis moved from French to Spanish possession; according to the Indians they both remained in Indian possession.

1766   Jonathan Carver was despatched from Mackinac Island, where Lake Superior meets Lake Huron and Lake Michigan, to find a route to the Pacific, which was thought to be not too distant. He wintered in what later was named Carver County. He wrote a widely read account of his travels.

1783   In the treaty ending the American Revolution, England ceded the land east of the Mississippi, including the future site of St. Paul, to the new United States of America. The Indians were presumably unaware of the change, there being no Europeans around to tell them nor, for thirty years, to remove the English flags.

1803   Napoleon, having forced Spain to give him their American holdings, sold them to the United States as the Louisiana Purchase. Thus the future site of Minneapolis, half of which was owned by the

Dakotas and half by the Ojibwas, was transferred under duress by Spain to France who sold it to the Americans while a British flag flew over it.

1805   Lieutenant Zebulon Pike, as an emissary of President Thomas Jefferson, visited various trading posts as far north as Leech Lake and negotiated with the Indians to purchase the land at the confluence of the Mississippi and the Minnesota rivers.

1818   Michigan's boundaries were extended west to the Mississippi, and its governor, Lewis Cass, came and tried unsucessfully to find the source of the Mississippi. A county was named for him.

1819   Colonel Leavenworth had a fort built on the land Pike had purchased. It was named after its designer and first commandant, Josiah Snelling, whose soldiers considered him a good officer. The fort was the northwesternmost military post of the United States and became the center for a large fur trade. Lake Harriet was named for the colonel's wife.

1832   Henry Schoolcraft discovered and named Lake Itasca the "true head" [Latin: ver**ITAS CA**put] source of the Mississippi. Joseph Nicollet toured the area and drew the first accurate map. A county was named for Nicollet but not for Schoolcraft whose name might have alienated children.

1837   Two treaties were negotiated with the Indians opening up the land between the St. Croix River, which is now the border with Wisconsin, and the Mississippi River, including most of the present metropolitan area.

1840   St. Paul was founded, known as "Pigs Eye."

1848   The first settlers came to St. Anthony, later to be Minneapolis. The first sawmill opened the next year.

1849   Congress passed the bill organizing Minnesota as a territory and appointing Alexander Ramsey as its first territorial governor. A county was named for him.

1850   The whole of what is now Minnesota had a population of 6,077. It included only fifty-three lawyers. John Stevens built the first house on the Minneapolis side of the Mississippi.

1851   A treaty with the Indians at Traverse des Sioux opened up 24 million acres at twelve and a half cents per acre, most of the Sioux land in the territory west of the Mississippi. Treaties in 1854 and 1855 opened up most of the northern half of the territory. The ensuing land rush increased the territory's population to 150,037 in 1857. Stillwater grew as head of navigation of the St. Croix, St. Paul as head of navigation of the Mississippi, and St. Anthony, later Minneapolis, as a lumber milling center based on the falls.

1854   The first flour mill in St. Anthony was built.

1855   The first bridge to cross the Mississippi River anywhere, a suspension bridge, was built between St. Anthony and Minneapolis.

1856   Minneapolis incorporated; it reincorporated in 1867.

1858   Minnesota was admitted to the union. Henry Sibley became its first governor.

1859   Alexander Ramsey was elected governor.

1862   The Sioux rebelled, feeling they had been unfairly treated by the treaty of 1851, that their reservation had been arbitrarily cut in half in 1858, and that payments under the treaty were going to traders, not to Indians. More than 350 whites were killed until General Henry Sibley drove the Indians all the way to the Missouri River. A county was named for him.

1863   Minnesota was the first state to raise troops for the Northern cause in the Civil War. In 1863 a Minnesota regiment saved the Union lines in the Battle of Gettysburg, suffering 47 percent casualties. It has been called the turning point of the war.

1869   Classes commenced at the University of Minnesota.

1870   Gas lights, using wooden mains, lighted downtown Minneapolis.

1872   Minneapolis and St. Anthony merged.

1876   Women were given the vote and allowed to seek elective office in school and library elections—among the first women suffrage successes anywhere in the country.

1881   Powers and Donaldsons Department Stores opened on Nicollet Avenue.

1882   The first hydroelectric station in the United States was built at St. Anthony Falls.

1889   The Minneapolis Public Library opened. The first electric streetcar in Minneapolis began to run.

1892   The Republican National Convention, meeting in Minneapolis, nominated Benjamin Harrison for President of the United States.

1902   Daytons Department Store was founded on Nicollet Avenue, today the eighth largest retailer in the world.

1903   The Minneapolis Symphony Orchestra first performed, now the Minnesota Symphony.

1906   Sixty-seven miles of road were paved.

1915   The Minneapolis Art Institute opened in its new building.

1925   Ford assembly plant opened, using hydroelectric power from the Mississippi.

1926   Northwest Airlines commenced commercial flights to Chicago.

1930   Frank Kellogg of St. Paul, United States Secretary of State, received the Nobel Peace Prize for initiating the Kellogg-Briand Peace Pact in which most of the nations of the world agreed not to make war again.

1934   The Teamster's Union struck, driving the police into hiding, and violence surged through downtown. *Time* magazine editorialized that if a revolution were to start in the United States, it would start in Minneapolis. The strike was finally suppressed by National Guard reluctantly called out by Governor Floyd B. Olson, the first governor elected by the Farmer-Labor Party.

1944   Hubert Humphrey was elected mayor of Minneapolis after organizing the Democratic-Farmer-Labor Party, still the dominant party in Minnesota.

1954   Open-heart surgery was pioneered at the University of Minnesota.

1959   St. Lawrence Seaway opened, bringing ocean-going shipping to Duluth, with a considerable benefit to the Twin Cities.

1961   Twins and Vikings commenced play in the Twin Cities.

1982   The Hubert H. Humphrey Metrodome opened for major league sports and numerous local activities.

CHAPTER 1

Science and Engineering

Science Museum of Minnesota

The seats are almost horizontal so that you can see all of the huge dome above you. The picture seems to be all around you, so much so that you feel as though you are in the middle. The McKnight Omnitheater is a scientific marvel for three-dimensional pictures. You are not watching the skier rushing down the mountain, it is you who is facing the steep drops. You don't fly over an active volcano as you would in an airplane, you go down into it, with the bursting fire and searing heat on all sides. That magnificent flower lets you right inside to sense the beauty and feel the curving petals. Each visit will become a never-forgotten memory for children as well as for adults.

The Search for the Great Sharks brings you face to face with a killer, lets you swim along beside it, almost share in gobbling the bloody chunks of meat. The world's largest fish, the whale-shark, can incite terror by thinking of it. It is the dread of divers even from a fragile Plexiglas diving shell. But you are swimming in the water, looking at it. Or you may watch as a coral reef in the far Pacific explodes with life. Not only do you see and feel and experience nature, you sense the impact of humans upon it, the often negative impact.

There is a full-sized dinosaur and some of his ancient companions. There are things of nature to be seen and touched. There are things of the future to be contemplated. At least a day is needed for viewing if you would see it all.

The Science Museum of Minnesota has grown over the past eighty years from a small, exclusive club to a great institution for the public to learn from active exhibits and dynamic programs, where the public can see the use of scientific research and the great need for it. It was originally in a large mansion with glass cabinets, trophy heads on the walls, and static dioramas. Now the Science Museum of Minnesota has become two buildings designed for its purposes with five exhibit and programming floors, research labs, classrooms, a library, the dinosaurs, and the wonderful Omnitheater plus, away from the city, a 400-acre nature center and a 250-acre field research center near Marine-on-St. Croix, just north of Stillwater.

It's a place of wonder!

Hours: Monday-Friday 9:30-9:00, Saturday 9:00-9:00, Sunday 10:00-9:00 **Phone**: 221-9403 **Parking**: Ramps in area **Admission**: Adults $4.50, seniors and children $3.50; Omnitheater adults $5.50, seniors and children $4.50 **Address**: 30 East 10th Street, St. Paul 55101

Pavek Museum of Broadcasting

Back in 1919 Joseph R. Pavek, the founder and curator of the Museum of Broadcasting in St. Louis Park, built his first crystal set and a Model T Ford spark coil transmitter. This was the beginning of his life-long interest in radio. Today the museum is not only dedicated to the presentation of antique radio, television, and broadcasting equipment, but in making the non-profit Pavek Museum an educational tool for people in the fields of science, technology, and broadcasting.

The museum contains thousands of radio sets, components, vacuum tubes, transmitters and receivers, station equipment, "ham" equipment, and apparatus for communications functions. There are primitive crystal sets, aircraft and ship to shore equipment from World War I, battlefield equipment, and spark transformers used to send Morse code signals, such as the S O S from the sinking Titanic after the unsinkable ship hit an iceberg. There are displays of more than one hundred fifty brands of home radio receiving sets used during the Golden Age of Radio.

Photo courtesy of the Pavek Museum

The Charles Bradley collection of radios built in Minnesota is displayed, as is the Jack Mullin collection documenting one hundred years of recording technology.

The Pavek Museum has an extensive library of books and magazines of the history of radio and television. Mr. Pavek has earned many distinguished awards and has become a nationally known authority and historian of radio.

For the children, the museum offers basic electricity classes on Saturday mornings. One of the most successful programs offered has been a workshop for fourth, fifth, and sixth graders, teaching them to produce their own radio shows using vintage equipment.

Come and share Mr. Pavek's enthusiasm.

Hours: Tuesday-Friday 10:00-6:00, Saturday 9:00-5:00 **Phone**: 926-8198 **Parking**: Curbside **Admission**: Free **Address**: 3515-17 Raleigh Ave., St. Louis Park 55416 (just east of Highway 100 off the 36th St. exit)

Museum of Questionable Medical Practices

Over four hundred exhibits are on display here. Each proclaims that it will do wonders for you. Most claim to cure a specific disability or disease; some claim to cure anything. It would surely be nice if they did, but none of them work!

There are machines to make you younger, machines to enlarge your breasts, machines to cure cancer, machines to prevent baldness, machines to reduce fat thighs. There is a marvelous electric belt that supposedly restores or increases the sexual powers of men. Many use electricity. Some have complex switchboards with flashing, colored lights and meters with moving needles and rheostatic controls. There are wonderful diagrams of how the machine works and even more wonderful before-and-after pictures.

Directions and General Remarks
RELATING TO

Mioxrl  Electric

Trade Mark

BODY BATTERY
NATURE'S VITALIZER
TO BUILD UP AND STRENGTHEN THE SEX-
UAL ORGANS AND FOR
Rheumatism, Neuralgia, Liver and Kidney Troubles, Lumbago, Constipation, Piles, Lame

Illustration courtesy of Bob McCoy

Bob McCoy has a lot of fun with his museum of quackery. About 5,000 people a year come to see his displays at 219 Main St. Southeast in the back of a restored building in the St. Anthony Main district, which is itself a fascinating place to stroll around, to see the river at water level, to visit the stores, eat at the restaurants, and, above all, visit the Museum of Questionable Medical Practices. But don't buy any of them, no matter how much you're tempted as Bob talks about them in his W.C. Fields look-alike manner.

Hours: Monday-Friday 5:00-9:00, Saturday 11:00-10:00, Sunday noon-5:00
Phone: 379-4046 **Parking**: You may have to walk a block **Admission**: Free, dona-

tions accepted **Address**: 219 SE Main St. Minneapolis 55414 (on the east bank of the Mississippi below the Third Avenue Bridge)

Bakken Institute

The Bakken is a collection of electrical and electromagnetic devices used through the years for medical purposes, starting with electric eels that were used by the ancient Romans and including a hand-illustrated parchment text from 1280. There is a nineteenth-century precursor of a pacemaker. There is a beautiful wooden cabinet in which a person could sit amidst bright lights and heat. There is an electrostatic generator and a coin-operated mild electric shock treatment apparatus.

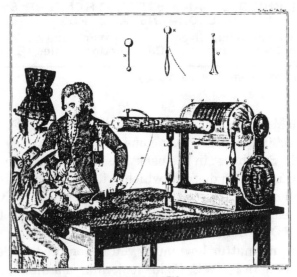

George Adams. *An essay on electricity.* 1799.

Illustration courtesy of the Bakken Institute

Wander through and read the explanations, and picture yourself being treated with each implement. Then realize that out of all this has come health and long life for many thousands of people. Notice that just one item, the pacemaker, has grown into a large industry in the Twin Cities by the genius of Dr. Bakken.

The Bakken also includes, amidst flowers and a meditation pool, a beautiful herbal garden of plants used for medicinal purposes. There are lilies of the valley, foxglove, lady's mantle, angelica, some fifty plants together with lavishly illustrated books.

The Bakken is housed in three stories of a magnificent Tudor mansion at the southwest corner of Lake Calhoun in Minneapolis, built by a young gentleman to impress a young lady to marry him. She didn't, and he stayed forever a bachelor.

Touring the house would be a pleasure in itself even without the exhibits. It has large rooms, wandering passageways, numerous wood carvings, interior balconies, and a large fireplace.

It is a center for learning, with books, medical instruments, and archival materials to research the history and applications of electromagnetism in the life sciences and to benefit contemporary society.

The Bakken was established in 1976 by Earl Bakken, inventor of the first wearable cardiac pacemaker as a private, non-profit institution housing some 10,000 books and manuscripts and some 2,000 artifacts, scientific instruments, and toys.

Hours: Monday-Friday 9:00-5:00, Saturday 9:30-4:30 **Phone**: 927-6508 **Parking**: Ample curbside **Admission**: Adults $3, seniors and students $2 **Address**: 3537 Zenith Avenue South, Minneapolis 55416. The museum faces Lake Calhoun; the entrance is on the side away from the lake.

The Planetarium

The miraculous basis for the Planetarium is a Spitz Model C planetarium instrument which was custom-made in 1959-60 for this 160-seat theater with the skyline of Minneapolis at the base of its dome. With it, over 2,000 stars, the planets visible to the naked eye, the sun, the moon, and numerous phenomena of the skies and the universe can be projected. It can accurately show not only placements of every object but their movements through space. It can be set to show the appearance of the heavens from any location on Earth on any date in 52,000 years.

To enhance the main projector, there are more than fifty auxiliary projectors so that audiences can watch a simulated launch of a space shuttle, or the condition on the surface of other planets, or the stately rotation of a nearby galaxy.

The wing of the Minneapolis Public Library in which the Planetarium is housed has a forty-foot-diameter projection dome that has been physically integrated into the basic construction design. There are several rows of attached, upholstered bench-like seats arranged in concentric circles around the projector with seating for about two hundred.

The Planetarium can provide various programs for different groups. For general audiences, there are shows on topics of current scientific interest as well as displays of the current night skies. School groups are typically shown the night sky as well as a choice from a library of space-related programs for different grade levels. College and university groups usually see more technical treatments of motions in the sky. Special programs for backyard astronomers and other groups are also offered. The programs are both produced in the Planetarium itself and purchased from other sources.

The Planetarium is forty-seven years old. The equipment, while excellent, is not the equal of newer models. Like a '48 Cadillac, it is a fine piece of machinery, but a '95 Cadillac would be much superior. As plans are developed for a needed new library, so the plans must consider a newer Planetarium.

Planetarium Hours: Daily 11:00, 1:00, 2:15; Thursdays 7:30; First Monday of each month noon; First Wednesday 7:30. Different shows at each time **Phone**: 372-6644, press 3 **Parking**: Lot on west side **Admission**: Adults $3.50, children under 13 $2 **Address**: 300 Nicollet Mall, inside library between Nicollet and Hennepin at 3rd St., Minneapolis 55401

Minnesota Center for Book Arts

The basic concept of the Minnesota Center for Book Arts was an institution for the paper makers, binders, visual artists, printers, writers, publishers involved in book making; providing a place where they could come together, where they could hone their talents, and where they could be instructive to the public.

Much of the public has little knowledge of the skills needed simply to produce a book. The Center seeks to display the book arts and learn something about them through classes, tours, and seminars, at various levels of participation. The Center was also intended to encourage the economic and cultural activity associated with books and to encourage the growth of the publishing and writing community.

Most of the Center's first year was spent in locating equipment, including an 1892 Alexandra hand press, the only one of its kind in the United States. Rigid specifications were set for the site, which, after checking out forty-five potential locations, was finally found in the McKesson Building in the Warehouse District*. The space, 8,600 square feet, was divided into areas for entrance/exhibition, press work, binding, paper making, library/museum, and administrative. An arrangement was worked out for Allan Kornblum to move his Coffee House Press and become a Visiting Partner, as Amanda Degener had done in paper making.

The Center opened its doors in October 1985 with all programs available except the library and the museum shop, which came the next year. It is doing well: its physical facility is unique in the United States; book artists have made use of it to continue their own professional interests, classes have attracted many people into the field, tours and exhibitions have educated the public, and the special artists and small book enterprises have come in. Over $750,000 has been contributed for the initial capital requirements and for program activity and development.

Hours: Tuesday-Friday 10:00-5:00, Saturday 10:00-4:00 **Phone**: 338-3634 **Parking**: Nearby ramps **Admission**: Free **Address**: 24 North 3rd St., Minneapolis (a half block west of Hennepin and the Public Library)

Minneapolis Grain Exchange

The room is a cavernous three floors high with balconies running around each level and a ten-foot-high electronic quote board at one end. A half-acre of hardwood floor is covered by women and men in constant motion, arms madly

---

*   See Index or Contents for separate article on this topic

waving, making rapid gestures at each other. It is the trading floor of the Minneapolis Grain Exchange, where for over a hundred years much of the world's grain has been bought and sold, well over a million bushels a day. There are tables around the room with various sized pans, each containing a sample of wheat, barley, oats, rye, corn, sunflower seeds, or soybeans for buyers to feel, smell, study, and even taste. The samples have all been recently taken from boxcars at country elevators scattered across four states awaiting shipping orders based on the prices developed at the Exchange.

It relies on oral agreements, thousands of oral agreements every day. In the flurry of buying and selling the large number of grain lots, there is no time to stop and write up a contract for each. It is necessary therefore that members maintain a reputation for fair and completely honest dealings. There are over 400 members, including processors, farmers, merchandisers, speculators, and terminal and country elevator operators.

The fast-moving oral agreements are written up later in the "Clearing House." In writing up the agreements, the Clearing House substitutes itself for both parties, thus guaranteeing that both sides of the contract will be carried out regardless of problems members might encounter.

The Grain Exchange has the largest "cash market" in the world, where grain is sold at today's price for delivery today. It also deals in contracts to buy grain for future delivery, called "hedging," useful as insurance for those who don't need the grain today but need the stability of knowing today the price they will have to pay on the date when they do need it.

Hours: 10:00-2:00 **Phone**: 338-6212 **Parking**: Ramps **Admission**: Free **Address**: 400 S. 4th Ave., Minneapolis 55415

CHAPTER 2

Notable Buildings

Basilica of Saint Mary

Built at the behest of Archbishop John Ireland, the Basilica of Saint Mary celebrated its first Mass in 1914, though it was little more than a shell and was not fully completed until 1929. With the Archbishop's seat clearly in the Cathedral* in St. Paul built at the same time, the Basilica has nevertheless been titled the "Cathedral" and currently the "Co-Cathedral." Mostly it goes by its more distinctive name, "The Basilica." It has many distinctions: it is the first basilica consecrated in the United States; its nave is 75 feet high, 140 feet long, and 82 feet wide, the widest of any church in the world when it was built. The building overall is 120 feet wide by 278 feet long, with 133-foot twin towers in the front, one containing a 3,000-pound bell, and, over the altar, a dome rising 250 feet. And it has a fifty-six-rank pipe organ. But these are only numbers.

---

*   See Index or Contents for separate article on this topic.

Photo courtesy of the Basilica of Saint Mary

It is most clearly a house of worship. The stations of the cross are recessed into the outer walls with figures carved into the marble. The confessionals are of marble with Latin inscriptions. The three rose windows are depictions of Mary, as are the clerestory windows on both sides of the nave. The sanctuary area is surrounded by marble pillars and a hand-forged wrought iron grille with engravings of Mary's life after the crucifixion. Above are statues of all of the twelve Apostles, exact replicas of those in Saint John Lateran in Rome. There are shrines and chapels along the walls.

The church's ministry also includes "Branch II," a neighborhood service facility with breakfast, lunch, and showers every weekday and with sandwiches and coffee Saturday and Sunday afternoons. It provides shoes, mittens, hats, and bus tokens. And it also provides child care on Sundays from 8:30 to 1:00. The church is very much a telling presence in its community.

Truly this is "A House of Prayer for all People."

Hours: 6:30-5:00 daily with a large schedule of services and liturgies **Phone**: 333-1381 **Parking**: Ramp and lots **Admission**: Free **Address**: 88 North 17th St. (Hennepin and I-94), Minneapolis 55403

Cathedral of Saint Paul

Construction of The Cathedral of Saint Paul was begun in 1906 during the archbishopric of John Ireland. He also initiated construction of the Basilica* in Minneapolis in the same year, both in Classical Renaissance style of architecture. It is 306.5 feet high, 307 feet long, and 216 feet wide. With the state capitol's* dome a mile away, it dominates the St. Paul skyline from its position on top of the Summit heights. Its seating capacity of 3,000 shows the foresight of those who conceived it and the Basilica when the population of the metro area was barely a fifth of its present population.

---

*   See Index or Contents for separate article on this topic.

Photo courtesy of the Cathedral of Saint Paul

The exterior walls are granite from St. Cloud, about fifty miles northwest. The interior walls are of American Travertine, quarried some ninety miles southwest at Mankato. The main walls of the various chapels are of Italian Botticino marble. The columns supporting the main altar are of Portora marble.

The seven grilles that surround the altar are of sculptured bronze depicting man's response to God's grace with special recognition given to Saint Paul, to whom the cathedral is dedicated. The Shrines of the Nations around the sanctuary are the national patron saints of the people who settled St. Paul and Minnesota. The stained glass windows in the chapels of the Blessed Virgin, St. Joseph, and St. Peter are the work of Millet; those in the Sacred Heart Chapel are by La Farge; the large rose window is by Connick and the angel series in the dome windows is by Weston.

The three oil paintings are the "Crucifixion" by Brewer, "The Descent from the Cross" by Lehmann, and in the sanctuary, "The Entombment" by Ribot. Statues of the four Evangelists are in niches in the four main piers.

There is a historical museum in the basement along with three assembly halls and a chapel.

Hours: Seldom closed **Phone**: 228-1766 **Parking**: Curbside and lots **Admission**: Free **Address**: 239 Selby Avenue, St. Paul 55102 (near the east end of Summit Avenue)

State Capitol

It is a magnificent, symmetrically proportioned building sited on a hill overlooking St. Paul and the Mississippi River. Designed by Cass Gilbert, when it was finished in 1905 it "drew acclaim from the entire country. Architects and artists praised its exterior, its huge marble dome [the world's largest unsupported marble dome], its self-supporting stairway, and its magnificently decorated interior," according to literature from the Minnesota Historical Society.

Photo courtesy of the Minnesota Historical Society

The Territorial Legislature, organized in 1849 when Minnesota had a population of less than 6,000, held its first meetings in a log hotel in St. Paul. Five years later the first capitol was finished and ready to be occupied. It was destroyed by a fire that broke out in 1881 during a heated session of the legislature. When the next capitol was completed the following year, it was already too small for the growing state. The present substantial Minnesota Capitol was an ambitious undertaking for a state which was only thirty-seven years old. Ground was broken in 1896. The cornerstone was laid in 1898 by Alexander Ramsey, former governor of the territory and the second governor of the state. It took nine years and $4.5 million before the building was opened to the public on January 2, 1905.

Sculptures over the main entrance to the Capitol greet visitors. The magnificent golden group at the base of the dome is called, "The Progress of the State." The charioteer, which represents prosperity, holds a horn of plenty filled with Minnesota products. The horses signify the power of nature, and the women leading them symbolize civilization. The group was regilded in 1995.

Works of art were commissioned by Cass Gilbert for placement throughout the building. More than twenty types of stone are used in the halls, stairways, and chambers. Handpainted arabesques with designs of grains and fruits grown in Minnesota adorn the vaulted ceilings of the corridors.

On the first floor, the allegorical story of "The Civilization of the Northwest" is told in four large murals at the base of the dome. Against the walls of the rotunda are glass cases displaying flags carried by Minnesota soldiers in the Civil and Spanish-American wars.

The Governor's Reception Room is ornately decorated with white oak woodwork and plaster of paris symbols of Minnesota overlaid with gold leaf. In the center of the room is an original hand carved mahogany table designed by Cass Gilbert and placed amid other historic furniture.

Hours: The Capitol is open most of the time. **Phone**: 297-3521 (recording). For tours; call 296-288 **Parking**: Ample unless Legislature in session **Admission**: Free **Address**: Cedar and Aurora Streets, St. Paul 55103

Courthouse in Minneapolis

She was built on Fourth Street facing north on what was then the south edge of the business district, hoping the city, about a quarter its present size, would grow from the river to meet her. She has a tower 345 feet high with four huge clocks, each bigger than Big Ben, that are surprisingly accurate, and a carillon of fourteen bells played on various religious, patriotic, and just plain joyful occasions. A very narrow stairway originally wound up to the clock and carillon. Later an elevator big enough for two small men was added. As the carilloneer grew older, rather than replace him, the carillon keyboard was extended to the ground floor.

She has a grand entrance on the south side of three arched doorways. The commercial heart of the city having moved to the north side, this grand entrance is of lesser use. It opens into a five-story rotunda surrounded by balconies and a massive stained glass window. On the capitals of the numerous columns are the "grotesques," small faces, some laughing, some crying, some sneering, some scowling, no two alike, a study in themselves.

In the center is the "Father of Waters," carved from the largest single block of marble ever quarried in Carrara, Italy, a copy of Father Nile in the Vatican in Rome. He is seated with his right foot in front of him with a well-formed big toe protruding. The toe has been rubbed for luck by so many thousands of passersby that it is as shiny as a mirror. According to the *Minneapolis Journal* of October 28, it was necessary in 1908 for the Municipal Building Commission "to create a new municipal office, called 'The Master of the Bath,' whose chief duty was to bathe the toe three times each week."

There was too much space to begin with so some was rented out for a chicken hatchery, a blacksmith shop, and a stable. Eventually the city and county outgrew it and it filled up as government buildings. Half floors were put in, an addition filled up half the center court, the courtrooms were divided in half, and the magnificent two-story gothic windowed City Council Chambers were squashed to one windowless room. It still wasn't enough. A monolithic, twenty-four-story, twin-tower Government Center has been built to the south for the courts and most county functions. It has a twenty-four-story atrium, a three-level parking ramp beneath, a half-block reflecting pool and fountains on the north, and a half-block forested park to the south. In addition, the School Board has moved to its own headquarters, the Health Department has acquired its own building, and the Park Board has moved to an adjacent office building. The jail which once required only half a floor now requires two very cramped floors and will soon be moving to a large new building of its own. But the "Courthouse," as most people refer to it, or the "Municipal Building," its official name, is still full, despite the half floors, smaller courtrooms, center court, offices, and squashed Council Chambers that have spoiled the grand concepts of the building.

Illustration courtesy of the Minneapolis Municipal Building Commission

The space in the northeast corner of the top floor was usually called "the hanging room." It was a plain, big room with a high vaulted ceiling, and with gallows across the south end, thirteen steps high. There is a legend about Minnesota's last hanging. A condemned man was brought to the gallows, hands tied behind his back. At the bottom step he turned to the sheriff and mentioned that the legislature was at that very moment considering a bill to abolish capital punishment and suggested that they wait and see whether the bill passed.

The sheriff shook his head and said that he had his orders and marched him up the thirteen steps, put the noose around his neck, and dropped the trap. But the sheriff had a tight budget, so he had saved money by not buying a new rope. It broke and the man fell to the floor unhurt. He was well versed in the Common Law, so he reminded the sheriff that if the rope breaks at a hanging it is because the Lord has intervened and the prisoner should be discharged. But the sheriff said he was bound by the judge's order, not the Lord's, and he sent out for some new rope, having the condemned man sit in the front row to wait.

In time they rigged him up again, and just before they dropped the trap, he laid a curse on the room. Then he died. Shortly after, the legislature abolished capital punishment and has never reinstated it. The hanging room wasn't used for some decades.

But then additional judges were added and a courtroom was needed, and the hanging room was converted to a fine, paneled space. The judge's bench, by coincidence, was placed exactly where the gallows had been. On the first day that the new courtroom was used, the judge died sitting at the bench. No one in Hennepin County is superstitious, of course, it's just that the judges were all satisfied with their old courtrooms, so it did take a while to find another judge. On his first day on the bench, a lawyer died while arguing a case. The junior judge was then assigned to the courtroom. On his first day, he collapsed, but it was only gastroenteritis and he was back in three months.

The courthouse is reputed to be the last American sky-scraper built without steel structure. Walls in the sub-basement are said to be thirty-four feet thick of granite and brick, tapering as they rise. At one time a judge with chambers in the lowest floor wanted a doorway cut through to his clerk to avoid having to go through the public areas. A simple job. He went away on vacation. When he came back in two weeks, they had just finished drilling through twelve feet of masonry. It did save his clerk some steps.

At the dedication of the courthouse Mayor P.B. Winston said,

> *"Reaching skyward may these walls ever stand as an emblem of justice."*

Hours: Seldom closed. **Phone**: 673-2150 **Parking**: In nearby ramps **Admission**: Free **Address**: Between Fifth Street and Fourth Street, between Third Avenue and Fourth Avenue

Old Muskego Church

A two-story log church, the first Norse church in America built exclusively for worship, it conveys an impressive sense of strength. It was built in 1844 for about a hundred worshippers near Milwaukee, high above some muskeg swamps. In 1904 it was methodically reassembled on the grounds of the Luther Seminary in the St. Anthony Park area of St. Paul on Como Avenue a few miles west of the Fairgrounds.

It had no heating for its first five winters and then acquired a wood stove placed near the front pews with a stove pipe circling around the room to radiate some heat. It was a rare church whose front pews filled up first! The altar is a strong expression in wood, dominating the room, directing eyes upward. There was no room for a pulpit or communion table in front, so the pulpit is reached by a very narrow staircase behind the altar, rising up above the altar, dominating the worshippers. The effect must have given awesome emphasis to the pastor's words.

There are small enclosures each with a chair on either side of the altar. One was for the pastor, the other for the "precentor," who led the singing. There is a choir loft in a balcony in a wide 'U' shape over the back of the church but with only benches; possibly pews weren't thought necessary for the choir. At first there was no music other than the a cappella singing; now there is a beautiful little pump organ in a corner by the altar.

Everything about the church is wood: the logs that make the building and the floors, the ceiling, the walls, and the pews for the worshippers. The altar is of wood as is the pulpit high above it. Even the organ and the baptismal font are wooden. The wood all came from forests near where the church was built and was split and sawed and carved on the site to fit the various uses. It has all aged well and has been carefully maintained.

The building also contains some interesting artifacts and pictures of when it was both the spiritual and social center of life for the settlement.

There are no services in the church these days, but there are weddings and baptisms and an occasional chapel service for the seminary students. There is a warning posted though that in the humid summer mosquitoes will flock to join the service.

Hours: Ask for the key at Olson Center, which is open until about 10:00 p.m.
Phone: 641-3456 **Parking**: Ample nearby **Admission**: Free **Address**: 2481 Como Avenue, St. Paul 55108

Target Center

It's big. It's new. It's modern. It's in the middle of the Warehouse District*, a large entertainment area. Target Center itself is surrounded by restaurants. It has so much parking that every spectator could come in a separate car. And it's been successful beyond the best projections:

- Over 1.75 million people attended the first year!
- The Timberwolves played every home game to a sell-out crowd of 19,006, and they weren't even a very good basketball team.
- The United States Figure Skating Championships drew a record 78,000 spectators.
- The Lipizzaner Horses drew the largest crowds of any of their performances in this country.
- The first indoor clay tennis tournament drew the second largest crowd in history, right after Bobby Riggs versus Billy Jean King.

Target Center can accommodate professional basketball and professional hockey, even though their seasons overlap. It can accommodate a full Ringling Bros. three-ring circus. It is adaptable to wrestling matches, individual singers and chorales, or to a magician and a marching band.

It has 20,000 theater-style, cushioned seats and 100 wheelchair locations, sixty-seven luxury suites, six hospitality rooms, and an elegant board room. There is a posh restaurant in the building open seven days a week, and fast food of every kind and style.

It has a sports and health club containing a full-sized Olympic lap swimming pool, two basketball courts, ten rac-

---

*   See Index or Contents for separate article on this topic.

quet ball courts, a six-lap-per-mile running track, and 11,000 lockers, all in addition to the auditorium area.

The Target Center is located a block west of Hennepin in the Warehouse District*. It is connected by two skyways to the rest of the city. It's a flexible, luxurious, user-friendly sports and entertainment center. Enjoy.

Hours: According to the event **Phone**: 673-1350 **Parking**: Ample in ramps to the west and north. **Admission**: According to the event **Address**: 600 First Avenue North, Minneapolis 55403

Foshay Tower

The Washington Monument was re-created in Minneapolis in August of 1929, two months before the depression began. Minneapolitans were proud of it. For over forty years, it stood as their tallest building, a unique building, their landmark. It dominated the skyline. It was the first thing they looked for when they came home to their city in the air or on the highways. Strangers were invited to share their pride. It was nearly twice as tall as the next tallest building in town. Now there are buildings nearly twice as tall as it. But the pride is still there, at least among the older residents.

It was built by Wilbur Foshay, carefully modeled after the original in Washington. It can withstand winds of 400 miles per hour which, hopefully, it will never have to prove. It was so unique that a patent was issued for its design. It is thirty-two stories, 447 feet 3 inches tall plus a sixty-foot

---

*   See Index or Contents for separate article on this topic.

mast. It extends four stories, sixty feet, below ground. It has 750 windows. It is eighty-seven feet by eighty-one feet at the base and fifty-nine feet by sixty-five feet at the top, containing 2,599,666 cubic feet of space. The letters in the name "Foshay" on four sides at the top are ten feet by forty-four feet across and contain about 900 sixty-watt bulbs which are lighted every night in the year. There is an observation deck on the thirty-first floor from which, when it is open, you can see thirty miles on a clear day.

Photo courtesy of Foshay Tower

In 1981, to welcome the hostages home from Iran, it was wrapped with a huge yellow ribbon, and in 1987, as a sign of pride, it displayed the largest banner ever installed on a high-rise building, fifty feet by fifty feet, to congratulate the Twins on winning their first World Series.

Wilbur B. Foshay was born in Sing Sing, New York, in 1881. He first saw the Washington Monument as a teenager with his father and developed an obsession to build a reproduction. He made his fortune in the utilities business, built his tower, then lost his fortune and the tower in the stock market crash of 1929. There were some irregularities which cost him some years in prison. He spent the balance of his life in civic enterprises for which he sought no recognition.

The tower cost $3.75 million to build and over $100,000 for the dedication, which included the "Foshay Tower March" written and played by John Phillips Sousa, three busts of George Washington by Hiram Powers, and a sixty-

six-inch bronze sculpture, "Scherzo" by Harriet Frishmuth.
A poem by Runion for the dedication (reprinted in a Foshay
Tower pamplet) recites:

> *Stark etched against the distant blue,*
> *Like finger pointing high,*
> *Thy flowing lines in tapered grace,*
> *Lead upward toward the sky.*
>
> *A symbol of that other shaft*
> *Revered the nation through,*
> *The vision of a dreaming lad,*
> *In stone and steel come true.*

Hours: Open April-October, Monday-Friday noon-4:00, Saturday 11:00-3:00 **Phone**:
341-2522 **Parking**: Adjacent ramps and lots **Admission**: Free **Address**: 821 Marquette, Minneapolis MN 55402

Courthouse and City Hall in St. Paul

Five Indians sit around a fire holding their sacred pipes.
Emerging from the smoke is the "God of Peace," thirty-six
feet tall, made of sixty tons of Mexican onyx on a revolving
base, the result of Swedish sculptor Carl Milles' vision of
peace. Since 1936 he has stood, forever impressive, in the
foyer of the Ramsey County Courthouse and St. Paul City
Hall.

In 1931 the cornerstone was laid. Departing from the
usual Greek and Romanesque architectural style and using
the Art Deco of American Perpendicular and Zigzag Modern, it was to become a wonderful example of architecture

Photo courtesy of St. Paul City Hall/Ramsey County Courthouse

during the Depression era. In 1928, just before the crash of 1929, a bond issue was floated to build the twenty-eight-story "skyscraper." One of the few good results of the crash and depression was the lowering of costs both of labor and materials with the resulting use of more expensive woods, marbles, and stone with a greater artistic and aesthetic interior and charm, so much so that the building has been placed on the National Registry.

In 1994 the building, which had cost $4 million, was given a $49 million renovation, restoring the original beauty and increasing operating efficiency. The renovation focused on the visible public spaces, such as lobbies, entrances, City Council chambers, and the Memorial Hall for the veterans of World War I. A new interpretive center was added at the concourse level.

Photo courtesy of St. Paul City Hall/Ramsey County Courthouse

The dramatic exterior of the Court House was built with Wisconsin black granite and Indiana limestone. The step-back of the tower from a three-story base and the dark windows and connecting spandrels cause the building to seem to soar on its bluff above the Mississippi River. Over the main entrance, there is a relief showing a police officer, a mail carrier, a newspaper boy, a mother and daughter, a blind man, an elderly couple, and a laborer, amid a traffic light, an automobile, and a fire hydrant, all showing the diversity of the city's life.

Above the relief is a towering statue of a female symbolizing liberty. She holds a book in her hand inscribed "Vox Populi" and "Jus Civile" ('the voice of the people' and 'civil justice'). Three small reliefs of state, city, and county emblems continue around the building. There is an eight-pointed star for Minnesota's Motto, "L'Etoile du Nord" or Star of the North. There is a washboard, copying the washboard on which Governor Alexander Ramsey* wrote the Territorial Proclamation, and a copy of the Proclamation.

A relief of a beehive and a scales are on the Kellogg Street side, the street named after a secretary of state who persuaded most of the nations of the world in 1924 to sign the Kellogg-Briand Pact, forever outlawing war. Other panels around the building are of a woman holding the scales of justice and a woman holding a cornucopia inscribed "Abundance."

Contrasting the stark exterior, the interior is Art Deco, derived from the International Exposition in Paris in 1925. Doors and metal work trim are of bronze and nickel. The columns of Memorial Hall have scrolls with the names of St. Paul soldiers killed in wars from World War I to the Granada Conflict.

The Council chambers have murals depicting the founding and growth of St. Paul from its origins in Pig's Eye's cave. There are scenes of Voyageurs, the Frenchmen who crossed the Great Lakes in their canoes and portaged across Minnesota to trade with the Indians for furs which had to be portaged and paddled all the way back to Montreal. There is a steamboat captain and the beginning of the railroad era. There are factories, Indians, farmers, slaves, and trains. A self-guided tour is available.

It is a fine courthouse. Its courtrooms are impressive and efficient; their support staff is efficient and friendly. It's a building to be justly proud of.

Hours: Usual business hours for its various functions **Phone**: 266-8694 **Parking**: Ramps nearby **Admission**: Free **Address**: Wabasha and 4th Street, a block north of Kellogg Boulevard, St. Paul 55102

---

*   See Index or Contents for separate article on this topic.

Hill Reference Library

The following information is from a pamplet provided by the James Jerome Hill Reference Library.

The Hill Reference Library [combined with the St. Paul Public Library] is a dynamic, user-friendly information center responding to the changing business environment and its dependence upon an accurate, up-to-the-minute business information infrastructure. State-of-the-art electronic databases create a "library without walls," where professional

Photo courtesy of Hill Reference Library

librarians help library users gain research skills that enable them to have access to vast amounts of information.

The Library's collection, which does not circulate, is focused on industries and companies in Minnesota and the Midwest. Information is also available for all national industries, public companies, and thousand of private and international companies.

Reference services are provided by phone for readily available business directory information or specific statistical data. . . .

In-depth Customized Research Service is also available for a variety of business subjects. Customized business bibliographies, statistical reports, and detailed public company data are available through electronic databases.

Document Delivery Service provides photocopies of information from the Hill Library's collection as well as the collections accessed through extensive local and national networks. The Hill Library complies with federal copyright laws. Delivery is available via mail or telefacsimile. . . .

In 1911, as James J. Hill approached retirement, he consulted with architect Electus Litchfield about building a reference library to be linked architecturally with a new St. Paul public library. During 1915-1916 the exterior of the Library was executed in the Italian Renaissance style, of pink Tennessee marble. Hill lived to see his great Reference Library erected, but died before the interior was finished. After Hill's death in 1916 his widow, Mary T. Hill, undertook the completion of the library, which officially opened on December 20, 1921, a month after her death. The richness of the Library's architectural design has been hailed by modern critics as "a high point in Beaux Arts architecture in Minnesota."

Today the Hill Reference Library is on the National Register of Historic Places and stands as its founder's most significant gift to the City of Saint Paul.

Hours: Winter: Monday-Wednesday 9:00-8:00, Thursday 10:00-8:00, Friday-Saturday 9:00-5:30. Summer: Monday 9:00-8:00, Tuesday, Wednesday, and Friday 9:00-5:30, Thursday 10:00-8:00 **Phone**: 227-9531 **Parking**: Nearby ramps **Admission**: Free **Address**: 80 West 4th Street, St. Paul 55102 (on the south side of Rice Park)

Minneapolis Public Library

The library is a prideful institution. It takes pride in its history, it takes pride in its collection and its collection's accessibility, it takes pride in its staff and its service to its community. It has been a central institution to the development of the city for over a century. It has been "stacked" with quality.

Some three million items are cataloged, though only about 16 percent are on open shelves because the building, more than adequate thirty years ago when it was built, is too small already. Service desks will quickly provide items from the other 84 percent upon request, and smile as if they were just waiting to help you. The range of topics seems inclusive. The on-line computerized catalog allows search by menu and submenu from any of several entry points such as title, author, subject, call number, or combinations of these. Staff can and gladly will help. Copying is quickly available.

There are ten rare book collections as part of the Minneapolis Athenaeum: *North American Indians, Natural History* including a rare Audubon edition; *Early American Exploration, Books & Printing; Aesop's and Other Fables,* largely 152 editions of Aesop; *World War II* with over 10,000 items; *19th Century American Studies* with over 4,500 books, manuscripts, and ephemera; *The Minneapolis Collection* with thousands of clippings, periodicals, directories, photographs, and archival records; the *Anti-slavery Collection;* and the *Mark Twain Collection*. It has fourteen well-stacked branches throughout the city.

The Planetarium* in the building regularly displays various of the configurations of the universe on a huge dome over comfortable seats, with a lucid, friendly narrator. It has a gift shop and a place to buy extras from its collection. It has a parking lot on its west side and, on the east side, which is the Nicollet Mall, there is a large, interesting, bronze, interpretive sculpture by John Rood.

Founded in 1885, in 1889 the Minneapolis Public Library joined with the Minneapolis Athenaeum, the Minneapolis Academy of Natural Sciences, and the Minneapolis Society for Fine Arts to provide a home for culture. It helped teach culture and citizenship to the flood of immigrants who came into the land. It stocked libraries in the schools. It helped with the skills and data needed for the growth of the Minneapolis business community.

Of the thousands of persons who have worked in and with the library over its century plus of existence, two can be singled out: Thomas Barlow ("T.B.") Walker and Gratia Countryman. Mr. Walker provided money, land, buildings, advice, and his collections of books. More than these, he provided his time and his energy and his inspiration, the same as he did for the Walker Art Center*, and as he did in most of the cultural beginnings and developments of Minneapolis. Ms. Countryman was librarian for thirty years, building the Library and personally assuming responsibility for making knowledge available to everyone and making

---

* See Index or Contents for separate article on this topic.

everyone interested in knowledge. She succeeded quite well, always doing as much as any one person ever could. In present days, purely as a volunteer, Harold Kittelson has been a similar strength.

The library boasts another achievement. In 1876, pioneering a long road, the Minnesota Legislature granted women the right to vote and to run for election to the Library Board.

There has been and continues to be a struggle between Minneapolis and Hennepin County over library affairs. For many years, Minneapolis was paid a fee by the county to provide service. But as the county grew from a few percent of the population to its present seventy percent, the county wanted more and more say, and Minneapolis feared being taken over. At present, through membership in MELSA, the metropolitan library association, they have arrived at a *modus vivendi*.

Hours: Monday-Thursday 9:00-9:00, Friday 9:00-5:30, Saturday 10:00-5:30. Special Collections close at 5:30 daily **Phone**: 372-6520 **Parking**: Small adjacent lot, ramps nearby **Admission**: Free **Address**: 300 Nicollet Mall, where Hennepin and Nicollet meet

The St. Paul Civic Center

The St. Paul Civic Center, including the Roy Wilkins Auditorium, the O'Shaughnessy Plaza, and the Arena, is a gracious, well-maintained, and user-friendly building in the heart of the city within a few blocks walking distance of major hotels. It provides more than 180,000 square feet of exhibit space for every type of use and function, from a circus to a religious convocation. It has twenty-one meeting rooms which can accommodate gatherings of from 25 people to 16,000 people. Parking is available for 1,630 cars.

Phone: 224-7361 or 1-800-627-6101 **Address**: 143 West Fourth Street, St. Paul 55102; or write The St. Paul Convention and Visitors Bureau at 101 Norwest Center, 55 E. 5th St., St. Paul 55101

Minneapolis Convention Center

Big enough for three football games end to end in one room, small enough for an intimate and delicious dinner party, and about everything in between. A five-course banquet, a major ball, another national Presidential Nominating Convention? All can be accommodated with more than adequate support spaces, caucus chambers, break-out rooms, classrooms, committee rooms, kitchens, bars. The huge room can be divided and subdivided without loss of comfort or convenience. It's all there and has been during the few years since this huge facility replaced the Auditorium, which was more than adequate for 1927 when it was built.

The convention center has 280,000 square feet of exhibit space, a 28,000-square-foot ballroom and fifty-four meeting rooms. There is a 900-space parking garage underneath and 8,000 spaces in nearby ramps. It is handicap-accessible throughout, including telephones and restrooms, and it is a rare building that has sufficient restrooms for women. Electronics and lighting are state-of-the-art.

It's on the edge of downtown. Since it is connected to the skyway system, it is "climate-proof," making it possible to go to most theaters, maybe a hundred restaurants, and all of the large downtown hotels and office buildings without wearing a topcoat in the winter or a raincoat in the summer. Neither rain nor snow nor humidity nor heat nor cold need bother the convention goer.

Three major hotels, the Hilton, the Hyatt, and the Park Inn, are all within two blocks by skyway. The North Star, Radisson Plaza, the Marriott, and the Normandy are not much farther. There are some fourteen restaurants within a few blocks including French, English, Italian, Japanese, Chinese, Thai, Vietnamese, Near East, and various styles of American. Five churches are an easy walk. Major department stores Dayton's, Neiman Marcus, Saks, and Wards, and a hundred or so boutiques, shops, and services are within a half mile. Access to the interstate freeway system is a block away.

Phone: 335-6000 or 1-800-445-7412 **Address**: 1301 South 2nd Avenue, Minneapolis 55403, or write the Greater Minneapolis Convention and Visitors Association 1219 Marquette, Minneapolis 55403

Mendota Bridge

When it was built in 1926, at a mile it was the longest concrete arch span in the world. The Twin Cities took pride in that. They took more pride in crossing the river at Fort Snelling without having either to go miles out of their way or to go down into the valley, take a ferry, and climb up again. It connected Egan, where many major corporations now have their headquarters, with both Minneapolis and St. Paul. The grandeur of Fort Snelling sitting proudly on its promontory was slightly negated; the convenience of people was greatly increased. It cemented the location of the Metropolitan Airport, the world's twenty-first busiest.

In 1994 the remodeling of the bridge was completed. It had been torn down to the arches and rebuilt with more traffic lanes, a bicycle lane, and space for pedestrians. Its approaches were turned to a spaghetti of cloverleaves and underpasses. Now it can handle more traffic with more speed.

The bridge is a pleasure to look at. It has long, sweeping white arches rising above the deep channel of the river. Any other style might have been a desecration of its setting.

CHAPTER 3

Galleries and Museums

The Minneapolis Institute of Arts

Over 80,000 objects from years of artistic activities are contained here! Among the exhibits are a 2,000-year-old Roman statue of Doryphorus; a moving photo of Marilyn Monroe; paintings by Rembrandt, Durer, Van Gogh, Goya, and Blake; French art, Buddhist art, African art, Pacific island art; Chinese bronzes and brilliant yellow robes. There are period rooms accurate to the last detail. And there is the magnificent Walker jade collection. It's a feast too broad to be described in a brief space.

It has become a campus. The Art Institute was first built in 1911 as a grand building in the classic Greek design. It was greatly extended in 1974

Rembrandt's Lucretia, 1666. Photo courtesy of the Minneapolis Institute of Arts

41

in a blending, modern style. The Minneapolis College of Art and Design, said to be among the best in America, occupies its own spacious and open building. The Children's Theater also has its own building, with a surprisingly high level of repeat season tickets, playing to sell-out crowds despite its ample seating. All the buildings are served by their own parking ramp, and a lovely park is situated just to the north. The architecture of the buildings has been carefully coordinated to make a pleasing four-block complex.

Photo courtesy of the Minneapolis Institute of Art

A highlight of the Institute is its Walker jade collection, in particular the extraordinary mountain dedicated in 1784 by the Ch'ien Lung emperor and possibly the largest piece of historic jade in the Western Hemisphere. Far more than imperial pomp, the carving is highly symbolic of the long-standing Chinese cultural values associated with landscape and nature. The 640-pound Walker mountain is the smallest of four large-scale works commissioned by Ch'ien Lung to have survived. The other three remain displayed in the Forbidden City.

Hours: Tuesday, Wednesday, Friday, Saturday 10:00-5:00, Thursday 10:00-9:00, Sunday noon-5:00 **Phone**: 870-3131 **Parking**: Ample in ramp **Admission**: Free **Address**: 2400 3rd Ave S., Minneapolis 55404

Walker Art Center

"One of the finest museums for the display of modern art in the nation." *The New York Times*.

The Walker Art Center, on Vineland Place at Hennepin in Minneapolis, across from its own Sculpture Garden*, presses the frontiers of art in all its forms. According to literature about the center,

In 1992-1993 its Education Department presented more than 1,500 public programs, including classes for adults and young people, literary readings, seminars, artist-in-residence activities, symposia, panel discussions, tours for individuals and school groups, and programs for families, educators, and community groups. The programs enabled more than 100,000 people to join in discussions stirred by Walker's presentations in the visual arts,

---

*   See Index or Contents for separate article on this topic.

film, and performing arts, as well as to discover for themselves the power of art.

The Walker presents more contemporary music, dance, and theater programming than any other museum in the country. In 1992-1993, the institution continued its long-standing practice of introducing emerging artists to the community, as well as maintaining its commitment to established performance innovators in their respective fields.

Media exploration of contemporary social and political concerns was a major undercurrent of the year's programs of the Film/Video Department. The second annual presentation of the Human Rights Watch Film Festival included films and videotapes from Asia, Eastern Europe, and the Middle East, while the touring program *Echoes of Discontent* focused on new politically oriented videos from South Korea and the Philippines. Works by major figures in contemporary African cinema were featured in the International Black Cinema series.

The nine exhibitions presented at the Walker during 1992-1993 featured work in a wide range of media by more than sixty artists from Europe, Asia, and the Americas; formats ranging from solo retrospectives to collaborative, commissioned projects. This rich array of exhibitions combined challenging art from emerging talents with work by established masters, providing both a context for understanding the new and a fresh perspective on the familiar.

All this, plus a large and acclaimed permanent collection, await visitors to the Walker Art Center.

Hours: Tuesday-Saturday 10:00-8:00, Sunday 11:00-5:00 **Phone**: 375-7600 **Parking**: Ample in nearby lots **Admission**: Adults $3, children 12-18 $2, seniors, under 12, and AFDC cardholders free. Thursday and first Saturday of each month free **Address**: Vineland Place, Minneapolis 55403 (on Hennepin at the southwest corner of Loring Park)

Bell Museum

The following information is from literature about the Bell Museum: "A bobcat stalks a grouse just inches in front of you. Sandhill cranes leap in their spectacular courting dance. From black bears to black bass, wild things abound in the green forests, cool streams and bright prairies." Three-dimensional dioramas put you very much in it.

Photo courtesy of the Bell Museum

The Bell Museum was founded on the university campus in 1872 and is now in a modern and pleasurable building. "You might also heft the weight of a record muskie, or marvel at Audubon's or Jacques' beautiful art, or find out what research tells us about vanishing songbirds. More than six new exhibits each year offer enjoyment for the whole family.

"Make tracks to the Touch & See Room. Pet a bear, touch a turtle, stroke a snake, and peek inside skins, skulls, and other wonderful things." Then camp out for the night surrounded by animals. Turn on your flashlight in the darkness and see wild things standing right beside you.

"Identify birds and wildflowers. Make a mask. Print with a fish. Use a scanning electron microscope. Try a canoe trip, an African safari, or a conference on conservation or genetic engineering."

There are guided tours, programs for children and families, field trips, workshops, special helps for teachers, and one of America's best natural history libraries.

Some of the research of The Bell has included: "development of radio-telemetry techniques to help track the movements of birds and mammals; the first convincing analysis of the evolution of feathers from reptilian scales; the elucidation of the effects of tropical deforestation on migratory patterns and distribution of Minnesota birds; discovery of the response of peatland animals to acidic bog water; and re-establishment of peregrine falcons in Minnesota."

Hours: Tuesday-Friday 9:00-400, Saturday 10:00-5:00, Sunday noon-5:00 **Phone**: 624-7083 **Parking**: Nearby ramps, curb on Sunday **Admission**: Adults $3, children [3-16] and seniors $2, Thursdays free **Address**: 10 Church Street S.E., Minneapolis 55455 (Church St. and University Ave. on the University campus)

Hennepin History Museum

Down the block from its prestigious neighbor, the Minneapolis Institute of Art*, the Hennepin History Museum is

---

* See Index or Contents for separate article on this topic.

-

doing very well and deserves more community recognition than it receives.

Photo courtesy of Hennepin History Museum

It boasts an extensive and fascinating collection of period clothing, tools, toys, and Native American objects. Innovative exhibits and programs highlight the close ties between the community's Native American and rural past and its urban present. It identifies forces which created and continue to define the city. It celebrates the survival of Native American cultural traditions and documents an array of work and leisure activities done by women. A new gallery will provide hands-on displays for children.

It is housed in the George Christian mansion which was begun in 1917 and finished in 1919. Both Mr. Christian and his son died in 1918, leaving Mr. Christian's widow to live on in the home until 1956 when she gave it to the Art Institute because a motel was built next door. The Institute in turn sold it to the Hennepin County Historical Society.

The revival style mansion combines late English Gothic and Renaissance. It has an old-world air of elegance reflected in the grand staircase, cut glass chandelier, marble fireplaces, walnut paneling, and cyprus floors. Half of the mansion's 15,000 square feet is used for storage and administration, the rest for public gallery and the library. Because the house is listed as a historical landmark, authorization for alterations is difficult so accessibility and traffic flow are not what the Museum would wish. In 1991 the Hennepin County Historical Society changed its name to the Hennepin History Museum.

Only about 15 percent of the collection's 15,000 objects are ever on display at any one time. Plats, atlases, and thousands of maps depict the growth of the area. The collection has amassed, primarily through donations, clothing, tools, toys, textiles, furniture, decorative arts, equipment of local businesses, business and personal records, portraits of local citizens, and the original diaries of Gideon Pond, one of the area's first missionaries who lived with the Indians on Lake Calhoun.

Hours: Monday-Friday 9:00-4:00, Saturday 1:00-4:00 **Phone**: 870-1329 **Parking**: Curbside **Admission**: Adults $1, children 50¢ **Address**: 2303 3rd Avenue S., Minneapolis 55404 (about a mile south of the Convention Center, a block north of the Minneapolis Institute of Art)

Minnesota Historical Society

"It is an innovative museum, a state-of-the-art research center, and a great place for a family outing. At the History Center, you can explore Minnesota's past through museum exhibits that feature large scale objects, hands-on experiences, and multimedia presentations. The whole alphabet is displayed, with an exhibit matching each letter. Hear vintage Betty Crocker radio broadcasts; touch a buffalo horn; enjoy films, concerts, theatrical performances, and lectures in the 3M auditorium. The Research Center provides access to the Society's vast collections related to Minnesota's past. The History Center offers something for everyone." So reads information from the Minnesota Historical Society.

The largest exhibit, a boxcar, weighs twenty-four tons. A No. 137356 is well used and well worn but ready to go back into service. You can stare at it from all sides, walk into it, study its couplings, imagine its cargoes. It's a mundane thing, but it's a real thing, part of our lives, like so much of the History Center. It's made a big difference in where we are and where we are going. It has moved Minnesota's #1 export, grain, out to the world, with tens of millions of dollars coming back.

Walk through *Grainland* and discover how grain moves through a scale model grain elevator, the way it does every day.

Learn about wild rice. See the panorama of a ricing lake, with an 1890s canoe, with 1,500 living wild rice plants growing since 1990. Do the "rice dance," breaking hulls with your feet to remove the grains. Watch the videos, look at the products.

See a movie with pictures of Minnesota things and with readings from her poets and authors, memories of the land and the people.

Sit on a milking stool next to a full-sized model of a cow. Climb onto a turn-of-the-century farm wagon. Explore a privy. See the ten-foot boat that took Gerry Spiess across the North Atlantic alone. Stand next to an 1890s fire engine.

Photo courtesy of the Minnesota Historical Society

Hours: Tuesday, Wednesday, Friday, Saturday 10:00-5:00, Thursday 10:00-9:00, Sunday noon-5:00 **Phone**: 296-6126 **Parking**: Adjacent lot **Admission**: Free **Address**: 345 Kellogg Boulevard West, St. Paul 55102 (A little south of the State Capitol, a little north of the Cathedral)

Swedish Institute

It would be hard to imagine a more splendid facility to house the American Swedish Institute than the Sven Turnblad mansion, built by a self-made millionaire. The mansion is filled with oak and walnut paneling, ceramics, decorated ceilings, and rare personal accessories of Swedish glass, textiles, and art.

Photo courtesy of the Swedish Institute

There are the wonderful Swedish stoves called *kakelugnar*. Each of the eleven stoves is a different design made of porcelain tiles.

In 1929 Mr. Turnblad donated the mansion, his business, and many personal items to fulfill his dream of preserving Swedish culture in the United States by means of an American Swedish Institute.

Minnesota's Swedish immigrants arrived in Minnesota shortly after Fort Snelling had begun its mission as guardian of the fur traders and settlers. They came up the St. Croix* river valley and settled near what is today Lindstrom, Chisago City, and the area known as "Scandia*," where the peaceful countryside reminding them of their beloved homeland.

Today the Swedish Institute continues to teach the history of these immigrants and their descendants, spanning 150 years. A tour of the museum displays the furnishings,

---

*   See Index or Contents for separate article on this topic.

toys, clothes, books, and photographs which were so much a part of their life as they settled Minnesota.

The Swedish Institute offers classes in the Swedish language. Folk arts and crafts are also taught. Films, special lectures, exhibits, folk dancing, fiddling, singing, and an excellent library and gift shop all add heightened enjoyment for members and visitors.

Finally, and maybe the best, a trip to the beautifully decorated institute during the Christmas season will be an event never forgotten.

Hours: Tuesdays, Thursdays, Fridays, and Saturdays noon-4:00, Wednesdays noon-8:00 **Phone**: 871-4907 **Parking**: Curbside **Admission**: Adults $3, seniors and children $2 **Address**: 2600 Park Avenue, Minneapolis 55407

Weisman Art Museum

"There is need for new values to sustain the morale of individuals in the days ahead. The arts are a source of such values and I want this university to play a leading part in instilling them," said President Lotus D. Coffman of the University of Minnesota in 1934, when it comprised a community of more than 60,000 students, faculty, and staff. The Weisman Art Museum was built with a major donation by Frederick Weisman for $3.5 million and housed $2.5 million of art donated primarily by him plus all the collections of the University Art Museum that had been housed in four classrooms in Northrup Auditorium. It opened in 1993 on the east bank of the Mississippi River on the university's campus at the end of the bridge connecting the two campuses. Its primary mission is the educating of students about art and making visual art an important part of their everyday experience.

Frederick Rand Weisman lived the first seven years of his life in Minneapolis and adopted it as his "hometown" until he died eighty-two years later. Other than a brief attendance at the University of Minnesota and various visits, he always lived elsewhere, principally Los Angeles. But his attachment to Minneapolis was so great that he took the name of a charming and prominent Minneapolis building, the Rand tower, as his middle name. He was one of the tens of thousands who love the place.

The Twin Cities have acquired a curious magnetism: many people are moved here for a few years rotation by their businesses; a surprising number refuse to leave when their stint is over, even quitting their jobs if necessary.

Mr. Weisman got into the produce business in Los Angeles in the Depression. In time he moved into his father-in-law's produce business, and when it was merged with Hunt Foods, he became president, at age thirty-one. In 1958 a uranium mine in which he had invested began paying off well. In 1970 he started one of the first Toyota dealerships in America and parlayed it into control of all Toyota distribution on the east coast, with sales of $650 million a year. He sold it to concentrate on art collection, which his wife had gotten him interested in. His acquisitions were highly thought of, mainly because his wife had excellent taste. He once said that he "put his money where her mouth was." By the mid-eighties, he had over 2,000 pieces of art and was spending over $3 million a year.

It is a remarkable building. Its facade of large, irregularly shaped and angled stainless steel plates, thin enough to shimmer very slightly, capture views up and down the river and blend the trees and grass along the bank. The lower levels are for parking. The principal exhibition level is purposely at the same level as the pedestrian bridge over the Mississippi used by students walking between campuses, almost forcing them to look in and see their invitation to visit the art. The building insists on attention and rewards its visitors.

Time Magazine in January 3, 1994 described it: "The smallish museum concentrates on 20th century American art, and the exterior can be seen as a tough, gleefully manic (that is, American) work of Cubist sculpture or as a giant brushed-stainless-steel popcorn kernel, or as a wizard's castle in some 23rd century fairy tale. Inside, where huge skylights bathe the galleries in sunlight, the feeling is serene but never static."

The museum contains all of what was formerly the University of Minnesota Art Museum collection as well as Mr. Weisman's numerous gifts, roughly 13,000 works in its permanent collection of American art from the first half of the twentieth century, including the world's largest collection of work by Marsden Hartley, Alfred H. Maurer, and B.J.O. Nordfeldt. There is art by Phillip Johnson, the architect of the IDS tower, the metro's tallest building. The museum also has strong collections of Asian, American, European, and Native American ceramics, as well as Korean furniture.

The Weisman Art Museum and the *Star* and *Tribune* provided information for the preceding section.

Hours: Monday-Friday 10:00-6:00, Saturday and Sunday noon-5:00 **Phone**: 625-9494 **Parking**: Ramp under building. **Admission**: Free **Address**: 333 East River Road, Minneapolis 55455 (at the east end of the Washington Avenue bridge)

Goldstein Gallery

From 1911 until 1949, two sisters, Harriet and Vetta Goldstein, were professors at the University of Minnesota charged with teaching art "that makes sense to people and is related to all aspects of home and family living." So well did they succeed that in 1976 a group of their former students insisted on giving their name to a new gallery attached to the University's Department of Design, Housing, and Apparel within the College of Human Ecology on the St. Paul campus. The Gallery "interprets the pervasive role of art and design in everyday life, ranging from what we wear to what surrounds us in our living and working spaces."

The Gallery's collection has three foci: garments, textiles, and decorative arts. Together they comprise over 10,000 items and have become an invaluable research tool for teachers, designers, and anthropologists. And they are a delight for the general public.

The 5,000 items of dress date from 1760 to 1980 and include the various accessories and undergarments used through the period. There are magnificent wedding dresses, stately evening dresses, and everyday dresses. There are hats, shoes, gloves, parasols, purses, and spats. There are dresses for infants and little girls. There are dresses by high fashion designers. They reflect not just a "material culture but the image of how we would like others to regard us, our social selves as well as our psyche." Clothes may make us reminisce or reveal something about famous people of old, their sizes, their very personalities.

The textile items include over 1,500 items of cloth in all its many variations. There are scarves, wall-hangings, doilies, cushion covers, saddle blankets, crocheted bedspreads, rugs, tablecloths, and towels made of cotton, silk, damask, nylon, braids, fringes, and lace.

The decorative arts, the third classification, is difficult to define. It's things: objects, baskets, utensils. Most items are functional, or began that way. They may be concerned with food or religious observance or crafts. They are pretty to look at. But more, they tell us about ourselves in ways that words will not convey. The Gallery's collection is extensive—one piece is possibly 3,000 years old.

Hours: Monday, Tuesday, Wednesday, Friday 10:00-4:00; Thursday 10:00-8:00; Saturday and Sunday 1:30-4:30 **Phone**: 624-7434 **Parking**: Adequate **Admission**: Free **Address**: 244 McNeal Hall 1985 Buford Ave, Univ. of Minn. St. Paul campus

Kerlan Collection

A researcher's bonanza: 55,000 children's books (7,000 being original manuscripts), galleys, or color proofs, one-eighth of the books inscribed by the author. Over 700 authors and illustrators have donated original work, and thirty-one translators donated their manuscripts.

The Kerlan Collection is internationally recognized as a center of research in the field of children's books. It serves those who love children's books, or a particular child's book, to see the actual artwork or typewritten manuscript or the actual handwriting of the author. It is administered as a part of the Children's Literature Research Collections at the University of Minnesota Libraries in Minneapolis.

Pencil study by Maurice Sendak for Circus Girl *by
Jack Sendak (Harper, 1957). Illustration courtesy of
the Kerlan Collection.*

A second collection is of dime novels, the Hess Collection: about 17,000 British dime novels, periodicals, annuals, and boys' books in parts; 1,000 American periodicals, 30,000 American dime novels, and 5,000 hardcover series books. About 7,000 items are on microfilm available to researchers. The collection is so vast as to defy words to describe it.

Hours: Monday-Friday 8:30-4:30 **Phone**: 624-4576 **Parking**: Ramps in area **Admission**: Free **Address**: 109 Walter Library 117 Pleasant S.E., Minneapolis 55455 (on the west side of the East Bank Campus)

Minnesota Museum of American Art

Jazz, quilts, embroidery, drawing, painting, clay, sculpture, puppets, masks . . . The Minnesota Museum of American Art proclaims itself "dedicated to expressing through art the unfolding value of the American multicultural experience."

Since 1939, when he wrote a column on jazz for the *Washington Post*, Bill Gottlieb has collected photographs of jazz's greatest performers. And he has listened to them play at great length in person and on records. The Museum displays seventy-five of the best.

An example of the Museum's activities is an exhibit which has come and gone: In The African-American Presence in American Quilts, the earliest pieces are slave-made quilts, which have been found in every former slave-holding state in the Union. One pattern, "Jacob's Ladder," was hung on houses along the underground railroad to indicate safe places to stay.

Drawing from live models, working with clay and with demonstrations, discussions and slides, drawing for beginners, drawing for sculpture, drawing with colors, painting for beginners and experts, painting abstractions, sculpturing busts with an instructor or independently with critiques, the refinements and niceties of film and photography, printmaking for clothing, all have been offered for fees at the Museum. Variations will be offered in the future.

Photo courtesy of the Minnesota Museum of American Art

One class was a presentation of contemporary embroidery in America, including the use of both traditional and nontraditional techniques in the process of creation. An eclectic assemblage illustrates the individual imagery of over eighty artists.

Hours: Classes as scheduled but hours are irregular. Suggest calling for times.
Phone: 292-4355 **Parking**: 19,000 spaces within walking distance **Admission**: Free
Address: Landmark Center*, Fifth at Market, St. Paul 55102 (across from the Ord-
way*)

Landmark Center

A contractor actually paid the government to let him do
the excavating so that he could mine the limestone blocks
and sell them back to the builders. The architecture is
reminiscent of a French chateau, with turrets, fanciful ga-
bles, dormer windows, a dominating structure built in a
prominent location. The broad open spaces are set off with
marble columns, balconies, and passageways.

It was dedicated in 1902 as a center for the federal
government and contained the federal court of appeals,
several federal district courts, the post office, the Internal
Revenue Service, the Customs and Immigration office, the
Secret Service, and offices for the United States senators.
The court chambers were lavishly done, the rooms paneled,
beautifully furnished, with fireplaces. Most of them are still
maintained for view. The post office occupied the entire first
floor and, like a true government agency, everything was
painted green, including the beautiful marble.

By 1969 the courts had moved to larger quarters, the
post office had built its own building, and the other agencies
had gone their various ways. Scheduled for demolition, the
building was rescued from the wrecking ball by Elizabeth

---

*   See Index or Contents for separate article on this topic.

Musser and some dedicated women. The restoration cost $12.5 million. They cleaned the outside, opened the skylight, scraped paint from stained glass, and refurbished the wood paneling. The magnificent structure now houses:

- A 231-seat auditorium for the performing arts
- The Schubert Club's unique collection of keyboards
- The Kegler collection of unusual musical instruments
- The St Paul Chamber Orchestra of national fame
- The Museum of American Art
- The Ramsey County Historical Society
- Resources and Counseling for the Arts and United Arts

The Chief Justice Room. Photo courtesy of the Landmark Center.

The fourth floor has the restored courtrooms and judicial chambers, more lavish than can now be built. On the third floor is the courtroom where many bootleggers were tried and where the Barker-Karpis gang, helped by Baby

Face Nelson, escaped while awaiting trial for kidnapping two prominent St. Paulites, William Hamm and Adolf Bremer.

Hours: Monday, Tuesday, Wednesday, Friday 8:00-5:00; Thursday 8:00-8:00; Saturday 10:00-5:00; Sunday 1:00-5:00 **Phone**: 292-3225 **Parking**: Ramps **Admission**: Free **Address**: 75 West 5th St., St. Paul 55102 (across from the Ordway*)

Groveland Gallery

The Groveland Gallery performs with great dignity and skill two functions important to the artistic culture of the Twin Cities: It displays art, and it assists others in displaying art.

The Groveland Gallery was established some twenty years ago in the Lowry Hill Neighborhood, where the nineteenth-century flavor has remained. The Gallery was fortunate in obtaining an impressive, century-old, Richardsonian-Romanesque mansion designed for Franklin Long. It is well sited on Groveland Avenue just west of Hennepin, uphill behind the Walker Art Center* and the Guthrie Theatre*, overlooking the Sculpture Garden* and Loring Park with the downtown skyline in the background.

The mansion itself is an object of art. It has beautifully detailed woodwork, beveled glass windows, and exquisite turn-of-the-century paneled interiors. It provides a unique and elegant setting for the Gallery's displays of paintings, drawings, and sculpture. Simply walking about among the art in this charming home is a delight.

---

*   See Index or Contents for separate article on this topic.

The Gallery represents the works of more than twenty-five artists focusing on Contemporary Regional Painting. Additionally it has a particular specialty in Contemporary Realism. Various displays include a wide assortment of landscapes, still lifes, and figural subjects. Among them are *Striker Bar,* a 10-by-16-inch oil on panel by Mike Lynch; *Leeks, Eggs, and Peppers,* a 17-by-33-inch watercolor by Robert Edwards; *Curbside,* a 26-by-40-inch gouache by Carol Lee Chase; *Nude with Bird in Mouth,* a 42-by-30-inch pastel by Lauren Stringer; *Pedestal,* a 27-by-36-inch pastel by Paula Nees; *Sunflower in a Dark Orange Window,* a 36-by-30-inch oil on canvas by Matthew Smith; *Tidal Situation I,* a 25-by-31-inch acrylic on linen by Anne DeCoster; *Applewood and Floors, Afternoon,* a 42-by-29-inch pastel by Laura Stone; *Culzean: Evening Light,* a 36-by-48-inch acrylic on canvas by Carl Oltvedt; and *Untitled,* a 64-by-80-inch oil on canvas by Larry Hofmann.

The Gallery presents eight exhibitions each year, with exhibits changing every seven weeks. At each opening reception, the public is invited to meet the artists. The Gallery also maintains an inventory of over 500 artworks ranging from small pencil drawings to large scale paintings. In its other function, the Gallery has helped develop many personal and corporate art collections and has provided art to numerous museum and university collections. The Gallery's services include planning collections, acquisition, appraisal, consulting, commission, and installation.

Hours: Tuesday-Friday 12:00-5:00; Saturday, except in July and August, 12:00-4:00 **Phone**: 377-7800 **Parking**: Curbside or Guthrie lot **Admission**: Free **Address**: 25 Groveland Terrace, Minneapolis

Banfill-Locke Center for the Arts

In 1847 a tavern was built by John Banfill where Rice Creek flowed into the Mississippi, east of Anoka. It was a popular spot for wagons on the long, wearying trek between St. Paul and the Dakotas on the Red River Trail and for travelers along the first Territorial Road. The workers in the sawmills and lumber camps, the soldiers and fur traders, most everyone found it a welcome respite, a place to socialize and gossip and exchange information about the Trail and the countryside.

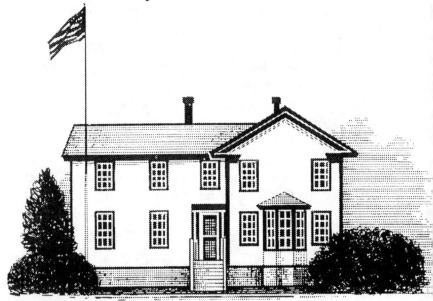

Illustration courtesy of the Banfill-Locke Center for the Arts

Banfill, thirty-seven at the time, was a mason by trade. He built his two-story building in the Greek Revival style. The inn section had two public dormitory rooms. There was a large dining room which could serve as a ballroom. There was of course a kitchen and an apartment for the Banfills.

In 1851 a store and post office were added in a two-story wing to the south and an enlarged kitchen and cellar to the west.

John Banfill became a prominent citizen, serving in the Territorial Legislature and becoming Minnesota's first state auditor. He moved to Wisconsin in 1861.

In 1857 the inn was sold to Alexander Ramsey and John Nininger and in 1912 to C.M. Locke, who used it as a dairy farm and summer home. Two porches were added and the interior was renovated. In 1967 Anoka County bought it and renamed it the Banfill-Locke Center for Arts, restoring it to its former beauty. In place of wagons and fur traders, there are geese and heron and an occasional eagle.

The non-profit center was chartered in 1979 with the ideal that arts close to the community are essential to public awareness and appreciation of the arts. Artists of all disciplines are encouraged to participate, teach, and exhibit. There are new displays every month: master prints and drawings from the eighteenth century, Chinese peasant paintings, and outdoor environmental sculptures. There are concerts, clothesline art sales, and holiday festivities.

Hours: Monday, Tuesday, Thursday, Friday, Saturday 1:00-4:00; Wednesday 9:30-4:00 **Phone**: 574-1850 **Parking**: On-site **Admission**: Free **Address**: 6666 East River Road, Fridley 55432 (at the Coon Rapids Dam Regional Park)

Hennepin Center for the Arts

Often called the "Wedding Cake," this handsome reddish sandstone building completed in 1890 on Hennepin near Sixth is Romanesque with Syrian-styled balconies.

Originally built as a Masonic Temple in 1890, its magnificent facilities played a great part in the cultural and social scene in early Minneapolis. But, with the exodus to the suburbs, the building's use diminished and only through a coalition of civic leaders was it restored for its present use, providing adequate space at reasonable rents for struggling arts organizations.

At the Center's reopening in 1979, 1,800 tap dancers performed in front of it on Hennepin Avenue, gaining a spot in the Guiness Book of Records.

Today its eight floors are home to twenty tenants. The Illusion Theatre performs in the eighth-floor theater. The smaller second-floor theater is host to the Lyric Theatre, the Cricket Theatre, and the Troupe America. There are also two restaurants, Minneapolis Dance Theatre, the Theatre de la Jeune Lune, the Ballet Arts of Minnesota, Arts Midwest, Sandra K. Horner Performance Studio, Minnesota Chorale, Minnesota Crafts Council, Minnesota Dance Alliance, Minnesota Dance Theatre, Northern Sign Theater, Brian Stewart, TDN Inc., The Theatre Exchange, Twin Cities Gay Men's Chorus, Twin Cities Vocal Arts, Very Special Arts Minnesota, Zenon Dance Company, The Creature Kumpany, Minnesota Shakespeare Company, Keepers Cabaret, Ex Machina Historical Music Theatre, and Zorongo Flamenco Dance Theatre.

Hours: Performances and tenants have different and changing hours **Phone**: 332-4478 **Parking**: Lots and ramps nearby **Admission**: Depends on performance **Address**: 528 Hennepin, Minneapolis 55403 (Sixth and Hennepin)

Lutheran Brotherhood Collection

The Lutheran Brotherhood Collection of Religious Art consists predominantly of woodcuts by Albrecht Durer, 1471-1528, and etchings by Rembrandt Van Rijn, 1606-1669. Each portrays a scene from the life of Christ or from the Bible. All have a deeply religious significance, all will have a deeply felt impression for Christians. They are quietly and effectively displayed.

Rembrandt's Christ at Emmaus. Illustrations courtesy of the Lutheran Brotherhood

Durer The Four Riders of the Apocalypse

"Formed over the past eleven years, the Collection currently consists of a few paintings, some ninety drawings, and approximately four hundred prints (etchings, engravings, woodcuts, lithographs, etc.) by old and modern European and American masters dating from the 15th through the 20th centuries," according to literature about the collection.

"For the past three years, portions of the Collection have been regularly circulated to colleges, seminaries, and congregations of the Lutheran Church as well as to other educational and cultural centers in various communities.

"Its goal is to establish a body of Judo-Christian art of the highest quality by the world's most renowned artists of all nations and periods. The Collection is restricted to works on paper [e.g., prints and drawings]."

Hours: Monday-Friday 10:00-4:00 **Phone**: 340-7000 **Parking**: Large ramps across both 6th and 7th Streets **Admission**: Free **Address**: 625 4th Ave S., Minneapolis 55415 (across 4th Avenue from the Government Center)

Bloomington Art Center

Believing that everyone has a creative spirit which is nourished by accessibility to the arts, our mission is to educate and enrich others by providing opportunities to participate in the visual and theatre arts.

So reads the mission statement of the Bloomington Art Center, founded in 1976 as a non-profit organization seeking to provide exhibition space for artists to show their works, learning experiences for all, and an outlet for the public to participate by volunteering and to view and purchase works of art.

At the Center, original art work is considered something unique and a very personal purchase. Buying original, regional art helps not only the artist but the community. Artists are only paid once, when their work is sold, unlike musicians, dancers, and actors who are paid for each performance. And artists whose works are purchased through a non-profit gallery usually receive more of the price.

In the field of education, classes are offered for children as well as adults, for beginners as well as the more advanced. Summer day camps for children are offered. In the studio, participants may paint, draw, make prints, and do ceramics and pottery. Students are also taught art history and the techniques of famous artists. The Nine Mile Creek Theatre Group for young people produces two plays annually. An Artist Registry Program has been established to enable professional instructors to teach their skills in schools.

There are several exhibition opportunities offered to professional artists residing in Minnesota and adjacent states:

- A juried competition which allows up to two entries per person
- An exhibition program in which a review committee chooses artists to show in the two or three spaces available in the Center's studio as well as Norwest Bank of Bloomington and the Bloomington City Hall
- An open "Call Exhibit" in which artists may exhibit on a first-come, first-hung basis

---

Hours: Monday-Friday 9:00-5:00, Saturday 10:00-1:00 **Phone**: 948-8746 **Parking**: On-site **Admission**: Free **Address**: 10206 Penn Ave. S., Bloomington 55431 (in the city government area)

Hennepin Avenue United Methodist Church

Ecce Homo by Ciseri was hung in the original church at Tenth and Hennepin when the city was younger. Three other works of art were in the Fowler church when it was agreed to merge into the present inspiring Gothic building at Groveland and Hennepin, just up the hill from Loring Park and across from the Walker Art Center*. Because of the great interest in these religious paintings, T. B. Walker offered his collection of religious art. Edwin Hewitt, the architect, designed a skylighted space for the collection. A catalog lists thirty-two pictures in the collection. However, seven of the listed paintings entitled the *Life of Joseph*, plus *The Assumption of the Virgin,* a copy after Guido Remi, have been missing since before 1940.

Between 1917 and 1970, the paintings deteriorated, and finally experts were called in to assess the collection and to determine which should be preserved and which should be discarded because of the lack of authenticity, poor quality, or unimprovable conditions. As a consequence, three paintings were removed; two were poor copies, one a fake, and one could not be repaired. Of the twenty-two paintings remaining, ten are certain attributions, three are copies, others are listed as "followers," artists who painted according to a certain artist of the area, country, or century, i.e. *Wedding Procession, The Assumption of the Virgin,* which are nevertheless of gallery quality. It has also been established that *Abraham and the Three Angels* was painted by Pieter Pourbus, a well-known Flemish painter. The Gallery also contains prints, sculptures, and liturgical textiles.

---

*   See Index or Contents for separate article on this topic.

By 1980 the most urgent repairs had been made, and more restorations were made by 1991. An endowment fund was begun and new lighting and humidity controls were installed. The Gallery is also fortunate in having Inez McKean Sauby, Phyllis Waggoner, and Irene McKean who have, among other contributions, prepared a complete catalog of the gallery with photos of all the paintings and descriptions of other contents.

Courtesy of Hennepin Ave. United Methodist Church

The present church was dedicated in 1916. The architect was Edwin Hewitt, who had worked with Cass Gilbert and was a graduate of M.I.T. He had studied the great churches of Europe during a four-year period. Albert Conmick, who has been described as the "greatest stained glass artist of his time," worked closely with the architect to provide windows which would enhance the environment of worship.

The church is an enduring landmark in Minneapolis, its tall, graceful steeple rising above the city, carrying eye and thoughts ever upwards.

Hours: Open days and for services. **Phone**: 871-5303 **Parking**: Curbside and at various lots **Admission**: Free **Address**: 512 Groveland Avenue, Minneapolis 55403

Plymouth Church Tapestries

It is large—16.5 feet by 25 feet—and covers a large wall in a large, delightful assembly room. Its theme is Thanksgiving, though a viewer's first reaction may be that it is Christmas. Displayed from Thanksgiving until Easter, it's done in Bayeux colors. The detail can require hours of pleasant contemplation. It was made entirely by the "Needlers" of Plymouth Congregational Church which is located on Nicollet just north of Franklin in south Minneapolis.

Illustration courtesy of Plymouth Congregational Church

The Tapestry was designed in 1970 by Pauline Baynes, a medalist of Surrey, England, and a specialist of the art and history of the medieval period. Ms. Baynes described the design:

> I used the possibly hackneyed Thanksgiving Party as the central idea, but it did seem to me that it somehow typified the whole idea of the Congregational Church, i.e., a getting together of all sorts of people of different ideas in praise, work, and thanksgiving in complete freedom.

> The central panel leads up to four church symbols, which in turn point toward the Dove, symbolic of all that is good, and toward which a motley assembly of birds flies from either side; this signifies the various colors and races of people flocking in congregation and freedom towards God and peace and unity.

> Each of the three panels, separated by symbolic trees, has its own emphasis. The left panel, Of Wor-

ship and Learning, depicts the building, learning, teaching, and worshipping that have strengthened the church. The central panel, Of Life and Its Renewal, illustrates the great fellowship feast that is for both body and spirit, that has united labor and contemplation from the arrival of the Mayflower to the present. The right panel, Of Freedom, portrays the parallel struggles from bondage of the Pilgrim and the Negro; a society of covenanted peoples must be free to worship and free to live.

The embroidery . . . is designed to be looked up at; the base border with its motto ("After God had carried us safe to New England and we had reared convenient places for God's worship, one of the next things we looked for was to advance learning"), foods, and discovered treasures from Holland and the New World has the most detail and the most intricate stitchwork; the side arches of religious symbols and the upper decorations are less detailed as the eye moves toward the Dove at the apex.

The embroidery is done on 17 vertical strips of Irish upholstery linen, in American-made Persian and crewel wool yarns. The 20 yarn colors are Bayeux Tapestry colors. Forty needleworkers [used] 25 different stitches in this embroidery. The needlework was begun in August 1971 and completed in November 1972.

A second tapestry of equal size, beauty, and complexity but with a different theme has also been completed and is hung from Easter to Thanksgiving. The "Needlers" are continuing their work, five hours a day, one day a week, on two additional pieces, both smaller in size, designed for the wall of a stairway in the church building.

The church itself is an inspiring place to wander about in, with many facades and passages that remind one of churches in England and Wales. It also contains the Howard

Conn Memorial Art Gallery with many sculptures of wrought iron and other materials.

Hours: Normal business hours and Sundays **Phone**: 871-7400 **Parking**: Large lot adjacent to the church **Admission**: Free **Address**: 1900 Nicollet, Minneapolis 55403

Nicollet Mall and Its Art Galleries

Nicollet Mall, the center of Minneapolis, is a lot to everyone. From Thanksgiving to Christmas and into New Year's Day it is a fantasy of lights and decorations, of parades and people, of bright shop windows and Dayton's block-long moving story windows that have had a different story every year for sixty years or more.

Along the mall, blacks, whites, Hispanics, Indians, Native Americans, and Asians mix. Voices speak English, Spanish, Russian, Polish, German, and French. "Minnessota Nice" is at its best, with doors being held and "Thank you," "Excuse me," "Have a nice day," and "You betcha" coming from all sides.

The Nicollet Mall begins where the city began: down by the river at Bridge Square, the Gateway. It wends its irregular way south with no vehicles except buses and taxis. The jay-walking laws are not enforced. The Mall passes the Public Library* and the open courtyard of the "NSP" building. It serves Neiman-Marcus and Saks Fifth Avenue, Montgomery Ward and Dayton's plus maybe a hundred upscale shops.

---

*   See Index or Contents for separate article on this topic.

Thursdays in the summer brings the Hmong vegetable stalls along the Mall from Fifth Street to about Tenth, laid out like a farmer's market amid the tall buildings, crowds examining the fruits and vegetables as well as the craftwork. And summer brings the Sommerfest with a month of daytime music inside Orchestra Hall* and outside in its adjacent Peavey Plaza, with pools and ponds and picnickers and people, followed by another month of Viennese music. There are ice skaters in the winter, rollerbladers in the summer, and bicycles and strollers all the time. Young people manage hot dog carts and ice cream stands. Windows display all the best of the world. There is a big statue of loons, the state bird, sitting among boulders with water flowing. There are insets with Indian sayings in the sidewalks near Twelfth and intricate tile work near Eighth. There is another statue near Fifth and trees everywhere. Down at Thirteenth, across from the powerful architecture and statuary of Westminister Church, beside the Hyatt, the Loring Greenway branches off, wandering among trees and benches and a shuffleboard court and teeter-totters and swings and picnic places and with flowing water all along until it comes to the fabulous Berger Fountain at Loring Park. In the park, people are playing basketball, soccer, and shuffleboard. Music comes from radios and tape decks and an occasional band. A thousand birds swim in the pond or take bits of bread from your hand. Huge goldfish swim in the channel and lovers lie in their isolation on the grass. Across a steel truss bridge are the Sculpture Garden*, the Walker Art Center,* and the Guthrie* and then the park land wanders off through Kenwood* to the Chain of Lakes*.

---

*   See Index or Contents for separate article on this topic.

Nicollet Mall stretches from the Mississippi River through the center of town to miles of continuous park land. Along a three-block stretch, art galleries are clustered together amid the aromas and sounds of Thai and Vietnamese and British restaurants. The art galleries offer a treasure of art. They are right next to each other but each offers slightly different insights, something for every taste.

Jean Stephens [338-4333] at number 924 features original art, graphics, and sculpture by major national and international artists. They represent Jiang, Ting, Max, Hart, Markes, Tobiasse, Byron, and Chin, as well as local artists.

Mumbles Gallery of Fine Art and Antiquarian Prints [341-2737] at 1004 specializes in British and regional contemporary original works ranging from realist to abstract.

Beard Art Galleries [332-5592] at 1006 was established over a hundred years ago by Harrington Beard, the founder, who specialized in original art by great artists of the nineteenth and early twentieth centuries. It has supplied art to many midwestern homes and offices, educating generations of its customers. It is currently and proudly owned by Harrington Beard's grand-nephew who has restored it to its original focus, emphasizing impressionism, regionalism, and realism. The gallery buys art, appraises art, and sells it, occasionally on consignment.

The Ancient Traditions Gallery at 1010 [372-9546] has an interesting display of Inuit art plus art and jewelry and native crafts from the Northwest coastal regions and from the Navaho, Zuni, and Hopi Indians of the Southwest. There are also annual shows of Pangnirtung prints and indigenous women's perspective entitled "Visions of Our Ancestors."

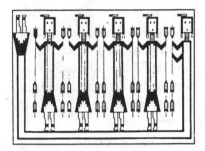 

The Kramer Gallery at 1012 has nineteenth and twentieth century American and European art. The gallery also specializes in American Indian artifacts.

Jack Wold [339-5191] at 1018 is an eclectic gallery, with oils and water colors, batik, pottery, etchings, and such.

Bill Daley [333-4922] at 1016 features illustration and calendar art originals.

The Mhiripuri Gallery [332-7406] has wonderful paintings, sculptures, and prints of African art. Rex Mhiripuri has done many of the prints including a local subject, the *Berger Fountain in Loring Park,* located just a few blocks away.

The Nairobi Gallery [375-1337] at number 1020 boasts East African crafts: jewelry, stone, wood carvings, Nubian baskets, and fabrics from Kenya and its neighbors.

Khazana [339-4565] at 1032 is more of a shop than a gallery; it specializes in collectible apparel, jewelry, musical instruments, and books from India.

The Vern Carver Gallery across Eleventh Street at 1106 is a family owned establishment begun in 1961 which displays Impressionist to Classical works by regional artists as well as very fine wood and ceramic pieces and seventeenth- and eighteenth-century prints and cards. They also do excellent framing.

The Dublin Walk, farther south across Twelfth Street and just past Dahl's drugstore, has Irish things: belleek china, Royal Doulton, Hummel, Kaiser, Claddagh jewelry and art, and Waterford crystal.

Gallery 416 is around the corner to the west on Twelfth Street at 416, specializing in contemporary fine art paintings and sculpture in seven media. The hundred or more artists deal in abstract, impressionism, realism, folk art, photography, and constructionism.

Hours: Most are open seven days a week from about 10:00 to about 6:00, sometimes shorter on Saturdays and Sundays. **Parking**: No parking at the curb but there are large ramps a block away, behind Orchestra Hall*. **Admission**: Free **Addresses**: All are in Minneapolis 55403

---

*   See Index or Contents for separate article on this topic.

CHAPTER 4

Gardens and Nature

Normandale Japanese Garden

An unsung jewel in a great city. A garden for the senses. Amid gentle hills, a little lake with little islets shaped like a crane and a turtle for longevity. A waterfall for its unobtrusive motion and murmur. Ginkgo trees, pines, juniper, dogwood, locust, crab with their delicate aromas and their varying shades of green, all with a backdrop of majestic maples and Norways. A Bentendo, a Yukimi lantern, a zigzag bridge, and a flat bridge for their quixotic Japanese com-

Illustration courtesy of Normandale Japanese Garden

fort. A thousand rocks carefully placed for a random blend of color. A wandering pathway to give constantly changing perspectives. Benches for quiet contemplation. Leave the world outside. According to literature about the gardens,

"For centuries, the Japanese garden has been a place of beauty, a quiet place for contemplation and refreshment of the spirit. It's a simple place—an artistic blend of water, rock, and vegetation. Takao Watanabe has designed an exquisite Japanese garden next to Normandale Community College just west of France Avenue and just north of ninety-eigth Street in Bloomington.

"In Japan, man's oneness with nature is the essence of his way of life. . . . The Japanese hold their gardens in great reverence—indeed some are located in close proximity to religious shrines and temples. . . . The gardens are divided into three groups: hill gardens, flat gardens, and tea gardens. This hill garden combines with pond and stream so people can stroll."

As you enter, there is a tall, granite pagoda lantern to your right and a Katsuga Lantern ahead. In the pond, as a focus, is the hexagon-shaped Bentendo with its curved roof and copper bells, a symbol of good luck, beauty, and music.

From the Bentendo the two islets are apparent, one shaped like a crane, the other like a turtle. The zigzag bridge protects from evil spirits which can only go in a straight line.

Illustration courtesy of Normandale Japanese Garden

"A Japanese garden is never simply a space that nature carelessly provided. It is always the studied creation of an artist. To the Japanese a rock is not just a stone or a piece of hard substance. It is a promise of reality beyond what the human eye can see. Japanese gardens are nearly flowerless, with monochromatic shades of green and the darkness of the ever present rocks." Flowers are used sparingly, as color counterpoints which come and go with the seasons and are even more appreciated because of their passing beauty. A Japanese garden is for the senses." A place for the soul.

Hours: Sunrise-sunset June 1-September 30 unless a wedding is in progress. **Phone**: 832-6000. **Parking**: Ample in adjacent lots **Admission**: Free **Address**: Japanese Garden. Normandale Community College 9700 France Ave S., Bloomington 55431

Minneapolis Sculpture Garden

There are more than forty sculptures and space for more. Some are huge, some miniature, some inspiring, some quixotic, all of them outdoors among flowers and shrubs and trees plus a glassed conservatory filled with more flowers. It's across the street from the Walker Art Gallery* and the Guthrie Theatre*, connected to Loring Park by the Whitney Bridge, a graceful ironwork span that crosses the freeway and Lyndale and Hennepin avenues. It is the final link allowing pedestrian access from the river, down the Nicollet Mall, along the Greenway, across Loring Park, over the Whitney Bridge to the Sculpture Garden and on along Kenwood Parkway to the Chain of Lakes and back along Minnehaha Creek to the river.

---

*   See Index or Contents for separate article on this topic.

There is a huge bright red, long-stemmed cherry poised at the tip of a silver spoon. A fine mist sprays from the tip of the stem over the cherry and down into a reflecting pond the shape of a linden tree. The cherry weighs 1,200 pounds, and the spoon is fifty-two feet long.

Photo courtesy of Minneapolis Sculpture Garden

The southern portion is the park's more formal section. It is made up of four 100-foot square plazas that resemble tree-lined, roofless rooms inspired by Renaissance and eighteenth-century Italian gardens. The elegant and artful design neither distracts from nor competes with the sculptures within it.

The area that the Garden now occupies has an interesting history. About seventy-five years ago, it was called the Armory Gardens, surrounding an imposing brick National Guard Armory with round peaked towers at the corners and formal gardens where farmers and gardeners would exhibit their bulbs, seeds, and flowering plants. But because the ground, a former lake, was too soft for the building's foundation, over the years it began to sink and slope and deteriorate and was finally torn down in 1933. A new armory was built on Sixth and Fifth Avenue, also a very military-looking building. It lost its military tenants, was used for the Minneapolis Lakers National Basketball team until they moved to Los Angeles, found some use to make movies, and then lay empty, taken over briefly by some Indian protesters. The county bought it to tear down for a new jail but the Supreme Court said it couldn't be altered because it was on the National Registry. So it just sits, empty.

The part of the garden that had been connected to Loring Park on the east was cut off from the park by highway I-94 until the Whitney Bridge was built. The acreage in front of the Walker Art Center* had become the Parade Grounds with playing fields and bleachers for high school football and amateur baseball but fell into disuse with the de-emphasizing of sports during the troubles in the sixties. In 1988 the Walker and the Minneapolis Park and Recreation Board collaborated to turn that playing field into the Minneapolis Sculpture Garden.

The wrinkled, skinlike surfaces of the figures in the *Bronze Crowd* were created by molding burlap around plaster forms of the human body and then casting them in bronze.

Hours: 6:00-midnight. **Phone**: 375-7622 **Parking**: Ample nearby **Admission**: Free
Address: 726 Vineland Place, Hennepin at Vineland, Minneapolis

The Rock Garden

In 1929 a rock garden was added to Lyndale Park at the northeast corner of Lake Harriet, a new feature for the Rose Gardens. Rock gardens were quite in vogue at the time; people were building big and little ones in their own backyards.

Theodore Wirth, the genius who planned and built the Minneapolis park system into one of the most extensive and beautiful in the country, as Cliff French did for the Hen-

---

*   See Index or Contents for separate article on this topic.

nepin County Park System, arranged for 350 tons of porous, weather-beaten, moss- and lichen-covered rock to be hauled in from Diamond Bluff overlooking the St. Croix River in Wisconsin. The rock had been broken loose from a cliff ages ago by frost action and had lain at the foot of the perpendicular cliff for ages more.

Amid the oak trees already there, it was planted with about 2,000 Alpine plants in ninety varieties, various sun-loving and shade plants, 1,000 native ferns in twenty-five varieties, 250 evergreens in fifteen varieties, and 1,500 native rock plants in forty varieties. It became the most popular part of the Lyndale Garden, influencing private gardens. But by the Depression year of 1935, the weeds had won the battle of too little money for maintenance and the rock garden was virtually abandoned. In 1981 a disastrous tornado struck south Minneapolis. The Rock Garden's oak trees were all destroyed, uncovering the rock structure. High school groups cleared away the debris, and donations came in to rebuild the garden. When King's Highway was rebuilt, fifty truckloads of the roadbed's rich loam were moved to the garden and used to build the outcroppings of the garden's perimeter. Volunteers from the Minnesota Chapter of the American Rock Garden Society assisted in the plantings. The result brought more donations. Volunteers continue to care for the garden.

In 1985 the Peace Bridge was built, patterned after a traditional Japanese bridge. The "Hiroshima Peace Stone" was donated from the destruction near ground zero of the first atomic bomb. In 1986 the "Nagasaki Stone" was donated by Hideaki Tsutsumi, a victim of the Nagasaki bomb. In 1988 a Peace Pole was given by the Society for World Peace in Chiba, Japan and dedicated by the Mayor Hitosi Motoshima of Nagasaki on his way to a United Nations nuclear disarmament meeting. The pole is inscribed on its four sides "May Peace Prevail on Earth" in Japanese, English, Russian, and Spanish. Every year, on the atomic anniversary date, August 6, the Women's International League for Peace and Freedom holds a memorial service at the pole.

Future plans call for a shady rockery, a recirculating waterfall, and pines and hardy northern azaleas and wildflowers blooming from April until October. But even as it is now, the Rock Garden is impressive and pleasant.

Hours: Open at all times **Phone**: 661-4806 for information and wedding reservations **Parking**: Curbside and lot **Admission**: Free **Address**: Next to the Rose Garden and the Bird Sanctuary on the northeast corner of Lake Harriet in southwest, Minneapolis 55409

The Rose Garden

Some 250 varieties of roses are all carefully arranged in beds between wild roses on one end and tree roses on the other. It's officially Lyndale Park but it's known far and wide as simply The Rose Garden.

It is part of a very large natural nature area, much of it given by Colonel William King in 1885 who named it Lyndale in honor of his father, the Rev. Lyndon King. The longest arterial street in Hennepin County, about twenty miles, is also named Lyndale. Ten blocks of median-separated Dupont Avenue as it passes the cemetery and Rose Garden is named King's Highway.

To the south of the Rose Garden is Lake Harriet, named after Colonel Leavenworth's wife, Harriet. To the northeast is the Rock Garden*, to the north, Lakewood Cemetery,

---

*   See Index or Contents for separate article on this topic.

beautifully maintained rolling greenery and trees. To the west, between the lake and the cemetery, is the Bird Sanctuary*. Farther to the west is the Lake Harriet Bandstand with nightly summer concerts, and Berry Park on the rolling wooded land between Lake Harriet and Lake Calhoun, which legend says was a neutral meeting place for warring Indian tribes.

Initially it was thought to be too difficult to grow roses in Minnesota because of the winters. The Rose Garden demonstrated that numerous hardy varieties grow well. The sixty-two central beds are planted with varieties of hybrid tea and grandiflora roses. Floribundas are primarily located along the inside fence of the lower area. Shrub and old-fashioned roses are planted along the outside fences. AARS (All-American Rose Selections) winners are added each year. The roses are covered against the snow from mid October until early April.

In 1946 the Rose Garden was designated an AARS test garden, the northernmost of twenty-three throughout the United States. New hybrids, numbered so as to protect the companies offering them, are evaluated for two years in the test gardens and, if worthy of merit, may be introduced publicly as an All-American Rose Selection. The test roses are located along the inside fence on the upper half of the garden.

The Phelps Fountain, originally at The Gateway near Hennepin and the Mississippi, has been at the northeast corner of the Rose Garden since 1963, featuring annual and perennial beds. The pedestal displays some of the ethnic groups who have participated in the life of Minneapolis.

---

*   See Index or Contents for separate article on this topic.

Hours: Always open **Phone**: 661-4806, which can be used to schedule weddings. **Parking**: Curbside and in a lot to the west **Admission**: Free **Address**: Northeast corner of Lake Harriet, Minneapolis 55409

The Bird Sanctuary

The Roberts Bird Sanctuary is a thirteen-acre strip of land on the north edge of Lake Harriet with the Rose Garden on the eastern end, the Lake Harriet Bandstand on the western end, and the manicured Lakewood Cemetery to the north. Within the narrow secluded strip, there are wetlands, wet prairie, open water, a lot of trees, and a pond. It is ideal for birds and for birders; more than 200 species of the birds have been identified, less of the birders. It is also ideal for exposing children to nature or for just ambling through.

Illustration courtesy of the Minneapolis Park and Recreation Board

You may not see the birds, of course, mainly because they don't want you to. But if you're very still, they may decide you're harmless and move about. And you can hear them even when you can't see them.

You'll surely find some mosquitoes, or they'll find you. Think of them though not as a pest but as a necessary part of the food chain, keeping the birds alive, particularly the purple martins and tree swallows who fly low with their mouths open scooping mosquitoes as they go.

Notice the vegetation; from the lowliest weed to the tallest tree, each has its part, each picks it own particular area whether it be marsh, edge of water, or dry land. Animals also pick their layers of the forest: insect larvae and moles under the soil; fox and chipmunks on the surface; squirrels in the trees, the trees converting sunlight into starches and sugars for use as food for the animals. It all becomes a part of the unique experience of walking quietly in the woods in the middle of a large city.

Hours: Always open **Phone**: 348-4448 **Parking**: Lots at each end **Admission**: Free **Address**: Northeast end of Lake Harriet. [mailing] 3800 Bryant Ave. S., Minneapolis 55409

Wargo Nature Center

The warm night skies may be filled with insects ready to carry you away, but at the Wargo Nature Center you don't have to hide inside. They have an aerial specialist to help fight back: bats, who in spite of all the scary stories about them, gobble up mosquitoes by the hundreds. The Center has classes to teach about these bats and how to build a bat-house for a colony of 200 mosquito eaters.

The outdoor learning center was designed to be used by the community. Interpretive programming changes with the seasons and includes topics such as maple syruping, bird banding, pond studies, apple cidering, insect investigations, and deer watches.

The interpretive center's two-story building is nestled on a beautiful peninsula overlooking George Watch Lake and is part of Anoka* County's 2,550-acre Rice Creek Chain of Lakes Regional Park Reserve. It is easily accessible from either I-35E or I-35W on County 14 (State 242) in Lino Lakes in the northeast metro area.

Native plants and animals can be seen, including muskrats, red fox, weasel, deer, resident birds such as pheasant and pileated woodpeckers, and a variety of migratory waterfowl. Various habitats include heavily wooded areas, wetlands, lakes, flood plains, and open fields. Animals can be observed from the comfort of the interpretive center, and self-guided trails are available for the more adventurous to traverse the community.

The Center also has a day camp program where children explore and experience the abundant natural world found in Anoka County's parks. Activities include hands-on fun such as pond studies, insect investigations, tracking, leaf printing, puppet-making, and bird-watching.

Hours: Tuesday-Friday 8:00-4:30, Saturday 9:00-5:00, Sunday noon-5:00 **Phone**: 429-8007 **Parking**: Ample on site **Admission**: Free **Address**: 7701 Main Street, Hugo 55038

---

*   See Index or Contents for separate article on this topic.

Eloise Butler Wildflower Garden

Thirteen acres almost hidden within Wirth Park, the Eloise Butler Wildflower Garden is named for a school-teacher from Maine. She was so devoted to flowers that she taught about them in her classes and wrote about them in her newspaper column. Her aim was to gather a sample of all the wildflowers of Minnesota into this one area.

A particular reason for selecting this place was the undrained tamarack swamp, such a swamp being the abode of most of our orchids and insectivorous plants so interesting in habit and structure. Indeed, most lovers of wild plants are bog-trotters and find in the depths of a swamp an earthly paradise.

Eloise Butler, 1926.

The sanctuary is bowl-shaped. It has wooded slopes and rolling areas. It has a bog which has been recently cleared of the choking loosestrife and buckthorn and has acquired a boardwalk. It has a trail winding for two-thirds of a mile in a figure eight among the plant and animal living spaces, called "habitats." There are forty-nine stations along the trail which are correlated with the guide book to provide detailed explanations of the various flora. As you stroll through the gardens you are reminded of the differences which shade, sun, soil, and water make to development and environmental life.

In the woodland habitat, mature trees shade smaller foliage, wildflowers cover the floor of the woodland, and in early spring the sanctuary is alive with beautiful spring ephemerals which bloom before they are shaded out by the leafing trees. By the bog there are shade-tolerant plants such as the state flower, the lady slipper, and the carnivorous pitcher which starves its captive insects to death. Add dozens of varieties of small animals and birds and an inspiration has been created.

Hours: April 1-October 31 7:30 to dusk **Phone**: 348-5702 **Parking**: Small lot at the site **Admission**: Free **Address**: Wirth Parkway south of Olson Highway, [State Highway #55] west side of Minneapolis 55422

Minnesota Valley National Wildlife Refuge

In the heart of Bloomington, extending for thirty-four miles along the Minnesota River to Jordan, is the Minnesota Valley National Wildlife Refuge. Created in 1976, the refuge provides a setting for wild coyotes, bald eagles, beaver, and many other wild inhabitants to coexist with over two million human neighbors. It is one of four urban wildlife refuges in the United States.

At one end of the refuge alongside the airport and the Mall of America is the Visitor Center. This is a great place to stop first to discover all there is to do within the refuge. The Visitor Center is full of interactive exhibits on the valley, its ecosystem, and its urban surroundings. There is an auditorium where the visitor can see a short slide show on the valley. The center also serves as a gathering place for many of the programs offered at the refuge. The fireplace makes a wonderful place in winter for children and their adults to listen to stories. Maps, calendars of events, and helpful information are available at the center.

Just outside is a spectacular scenic overlook of the Minnesota Valley. A short but steep trail going down toward the river leads off from the center.

With its proximity to Fort Snelling one can just imagine the traders, settlers, and Indians walking along. There are eight other areas within the refuge to explore. Five of these have public facilities, and the other three are waiting to be developed.

The Bass Ponds Environmental Study Area was originally used to breed fish for stocking the Minnesota lakes. This area is now open to schools and visitors with a special interest in nature and water management. There is a half-mile self-guided trail.

Long Meadow Lake contains 2,200 acres of marshes, fields, bluffs, and bottomlands which are accessible by five miles of hiking and cross-country ski trails. Black Dog Preserve is a wonderful place to observe migrating waterfowl from an observation area. There is a two-mile hiking swamp which contains 2,400 acres of marsh, bottomlands, hardwoods, and oak savannah. There are thirteen miles of hiking, cross-country skiing, horseback-riding, and biking trails.

Hours: Visitors Center April-December Tuesday-Sunday 9:00-9:00; January-March Tuesday, Friday, Saturday, Sunday 9:00-5:00; Wednesday and Thursday 9:00-9:00 Call for group appointments. **Phone**: 335-2323 **Parking**: On-site **Admission**: Free **Address**: 3815 East 80th Street, Bloomington 55425. From I-494 exit on 34th Avenue, turn left at the Holiday Inn, drive a quarter mile to the Visitor Center entrance on the right.

CHAPTER 5

Neighborhoods and Places

Anoka

Anoka is located on the old neutral grounds between the feuding Dakota (Sioux) and Ojibwe (Chippewa) Indians. The Dakota word for the area is *A-No-Ka-Tan-Han*, meaning "on both sides of the river." The Chippewa word for the area is *An-O-Kay*, meaning "work." Early settlers thus derived the name Anoka for this active city on both sides of the Rum River. The river got its name from the Indians, the reason for the name is not known.

The Eagle Scouts have laid out the Purple Line as a two-hour, four-mile, walking tour of twenty-five places of interest, including a former match factory, several historic houses, a dam, and a century-old green ash tree. Start at the Colonial House, a fine museum at Third and Monroe (a block south of Main), and pick up a pamphlet as an excellent guide for the walk.

Photo courtesy of Anoka County Historical Society

Anoka is said to be the Halloween Capital of the World because it was the first city to hold a big party for the children, motivated partly by giving the kids a good time but mostly to get them off the streets where Halloween was celebrated by rampant vandalism. Anoka's annual football game with its arch-rival is therefore played in the Pumpkin Bowl. And its football team is known as the "Tornado" because of a devastating storm that swept down Main Street in 1939.

Anoka County has a well-developed 8,000-acre park system anchored by Bunker Hills, just north of the Coon Rapids Dam in the Mississippi. Its 1,600 acres, two golf courses, a pool with waves, a large picnic area, and miles of hiking trails, horse trails, and ski trails give it something for everyone. The Rice Creek Chain of Lakes to the east offers boating, swimming, and fishing among its additional, numerous facilities including the Wargo Nature Center*.

Hours: [For Colonial Hall] Tuesday-Friday 12:30-4:00 **Phone**: 421-0600 **Parking**: In area **Admission**: [Colonial Hall]: Free **Address**: [Colonial Hall]: 1900 Third Avenue South, Anoka 55303

Carver

The Carver County Historical Society provides the following information:

Imagine what it would be like to walk with the Dakota Indians. . . to see your town and ancestors when they were young. . . to endure the hardships of early farm life. The Carver County Historical Society's volunteers and staff can help you discover a wealth of information, artifacts, and stories which illuminate the life of another era.

"The Dakota did not pretend to keep a record of time for any great number of years, and few of the older ones knew exactly their own ages; but long after the dates were lost, the facts themselves might be carefully preserved in memory. I have heard all the vicissitudes of a battle . . . minutely and graphi-

* See Index or Contents for separate article on this topic.

cally described, when the narrator could neither tell nor guess within hundreds of years of the time when the battle was fought." Samuel W. Pond *The Dakota or Sioux in Minnesota as they were in 1834.*

Since its formation in 1940, the Carver County Historical Society has been dedicated to sharing and preserving knowledge of the county's history. The museum in Waconia houses a rich and continually expanding collection of 12,000 artifacts, including early agricultural and carpentry tools, pioneer household items, Native American artifacts, Swedish and German Reading Society collections, and thousands of photographs.

Deforestation brought by farming gradually changed the area's Big Woods to fields. Isaac Lewis, an instrumental merchant of Watertown, remembered the wilderness townsite of 1857 as "The heart of the Big Woods, where butternut, basswood, ash, oak, maple, and other kinds of timber was thick. It came as near to being the happy land of Canaan, flowing with milk and honey, as any on earth." *Memoirs of Isaac Lewis, 1892.*

The museum also serves as a regional research facility, providing access to letters, diaries, maps, and census records. The public makes frequent use of the microfilmed collection of all newspapers published in the county from 1862 to the present. The staff and volunteers are now compiling a comprehensive index of the events and people described in these.

Jonathan Carver is considered the first American explorer to have seen St. Anthony Falls while he was exploring through the area.

Hours: Wednesday, Thursday, Friday 9:30-4:30; Sunday and Monday 1:00-4:30; Tuesday 9:30-9:00 **Phone**: 442-4234 **Parking**: Ample **Admission**: Free **Address**: 119 Cherry St., Waconia 55387

Hastings

According to the Hastings Chamber of Commerce, "The Dakota Indians called the area O-wo-bop-te, meaning 'the place to dig turnips.' When supply boats headed for Fort Snelling were stopped here by low water in 1819, Lt. W.G. Oliver was sent down with a detachment of soldiers to guard the provisions for the winter. The detachment built a log cabin in a grove of trees, giving the place a name which stuck for thirty-four years, 'Oliver's Grove.'"

In 1853 the townsite was renamed. Names were placed in a hat by the four original founders, Alexis Bailly and his son, Henry Sibley, and Alexander Faribault, and the middle name of Henry Hastings Sibley was drawn. They then platted and sold lots. The city was incorporated in 1857 with a population of 1,916, two hundred more than nearby St. Paul.

Hastings is located at Lock and Dam #2 at the confluence of the Vermillion River on the west and the St. Croix River on the east. The city hugs the river so closely that the approach for its first bridge, in 1895, had to be spiraled down to the street or it would have crossed over the business section. The result, the "spiral bridge," gave Hastings its identity for many decades; people would drive miles out of their way just to see it, until the bridge became inadequate for the traffic.

Hastings is also known for its twenty-eight largely Victorian mansions and thirty-five commercial buildings all on the National Register, most built in the 1870s and maintained substantially in their original condition. They can be visited via walking tour; a map and descriptions available at most stores.

The best kept secret of Hastings is the Vermillion Falls on East Twenty-first Street, a beautiful cascade surrounded by a friendly park.

Scandia

The home of the first Swedish settlers in Minnesota is an area of lush farms, blue lakes, and about a century and a half of history. After large tracts of land were acquired from the Indians, advertisements in northern Europe proclaimed that land in Minnesota was fertile, cheap, and beautiful with the same lakes and hills as Sweden. A clinching point was that in Minnesota there was no caste system, no hierarchy; a man could be whatever he could make of himself.

There were very few doctors in the Territory, but the developers turned this into a blessing by saying everyone was so healthy there was no need for doctors. The response was predictable. No one mentioned how lonely it might be that far from home or how cold, nor would it have dissuaded very many.

Gammelgarden, or "ancient garden," is an eleven-acre site on Highway 97 east of Forest Lake enclosed by Swedish log fencing and including six structures from the last century. There is a log church and a log parson-  age, an 1855 immigrant's log house with its barn and corncrib, and a vacation "stuga." Besides being open to the public from May to October on Friday, Saturday, and Sunday, noon to 4:00, the area is used for the traditional Swedish celebrations of "Midsummer" in June and the "Lucia" of light during the darkest days of December.

Marine-on-St. Croix is a pleasant place up river from Stillwater. There is a well-organized effort to preserve its history: the 1888 Village Hall, the old red bridge, the general store, the dam, and the river's first sawmill which gave the area its start. The effort has won a place in the National Register's Historic District.

The Stone House Museum at Oak and Fifth Street in Marine-on-St. Croix is the former townhall built in 1872 from local sandstone. It contains artifacts from the early Swedish immigrants and settlers from New England. It's open from July 4th through Labor Day on Saturday and Sunday from 2:00 to 5:00.

Just north of Marine-on-St. Croix is the 1,300-acre William J. O'Brien State Park, replete with hiking and skiing trails, campgrounds for both individuals and groups, and with a canoe base on the beautiful St. Croix*. It also has swimming in its enclosed Lake Alice and an Interpretive Center with various displays and with naturalists available to explain and answer questions.

---

*   See Index or Contents for separate article on this topic.

Edina

In the beginning, Minnehaha* Creek, "Laughing Water," emptied the water of Lake Minnetonka,* "Big Water," into the Mississippi River,* "Big River," in a steady stream of good volume. About three-fourths of the way along, it went over a falls. In 1857 Andrew Craik, fresh from Edinburgh, Scotland, built a mill at the falls. In honor of his hometown, he named it Edina Mills. The mill did well, grinding grain for settlers and Indians, taking a tenth of the product. Homes were built and settlers came, attracted by good land at $8.50 an acre.

Photo courtesy of Edina Historical Society

---

*   See Index or Contents for separate article on this topic.

By 1886 Edina's population had grown to 485! But then a dam was built at Gray's Bay to control the water level of Minnetonka, and the steady flow of water to the mill was reduced. They tried a turbine, which is now at Arneson Acres, 4711 West Seventieth Street, along with a beautiful fourteen-acre garden and a museum of hundreds of historical items. But it wasn't enough, and the mill had to close. Edina became a sleepy farm community threatened with annexation by its growing neighbor, Minneapolis. In due course the Como-Harriet trolley line was built out around Lake Harriet to France Avenue and Fiftieth Street, allowing a suburban development in the Morningside section of Edina. It eventually seceded from Edina because the Edina farmers wouldn't build roads for its urban residents.

For a fee, Morningside pumped its sewage into the Minneapolis disposal system. In 1953, after twenty years at the same fee, Minneapolis proposed a raise. Morningside refused. When Minneapolis City Engineer Hugo Erickson was asked what would happen if Minneapolis just closed the sewer gates, he responded, "It would raise quite a stink in Morningside." A compromise was worked out. Some years later, Morningside returned to Edina, its streets all paved.

In 1922 Sam Thorpe bought 300 acres near the Edina mill and platted out the Country Club Addition with a golf course, country club, and 550 homesites, the first such planned residential community in the Upper Midwest. It was marketed as a "high- class" place and grew rapidly, with substantial homes now worth an average of over $400,000.

In the 1960s Daytons, Minneapolis' large and respected department store, anchor of Dayton Hudson, promoted Southdale in southeastern Edina, the world's first modern indoor shopping mall enclosing a hundred or so shops and boutiques anchored by four large stores at the corners, a plan now copied all over the country. It was a great benefit to the consumers and a sorrow to the small merchants, as

Wal-Mart is today. Southdale has continued to succeed and expand, even with nearby Mall of America and its Camp Snoopy*, and a substantial commercial area has grown up around it, giving Edina an excellent tax base. Southdale has been replicated around the Twin Cities in a series of "Dales."

With its location, its amenities, its excellent schools, many consider Edina "the" place to live in the Minneapolis area.

Minnetonka

Minnetonka is a name coined by Governor Alexander Ramsey from the Ojibway words *minne* for water and *tonka* for big. And it is. It has nearly one hundred miles of shoreline, some of it selling for more than $150 a front *inch,* some of it quite reasonable. Every part of it is beautiful. It is actually about a dozen lakes with very irregular shorelines and lots of bays hooked together, partly by nature, partly by people. Only two or three of the bays are very big, and on a summer weekend thay are apt to be covered with racing sailboats. There are several islands, mostly given over to parks. It's possible to have a house with the front porch overlooking one bay and the back porch overlooking another. It's possible to be on the lake and be only twelve miles from downtown Minneapolis by a direct freeway. And it's possible to be twenty- four miles from Minneapolis and still be on the lake. There are many municipalities and three

---

*   See Index or Contents for separate article on this topic.

small cities on the lake: Wayzata* at the north, Excelsior* at the south, and Mound at the west.

The swimming is good, with mostly sand beaches, as are the water skiing and water sledding, some say too good for the noise they make. The ice boating is great until there is too much snow. The snowmobiling is good but a little dangerous because of occasional thin ice. The fishing is good in almost all of the bays, as the DNR stocks them with walleyes. The sailing is excellent and there is a lot of it. Often there are races with boats from other inland waters, particularly White Bear Lake* close to St. Paul and equally attractive though somewhat smaller. Maybe the greatest activity of all at "the lake," as it is universally referred to, is just sitting and looking.

There are of course restaurants, some with marinas, and there are dinner-excursion boats. There are country clubs. One has a golf course from which a bay of the lake is visible from every hole.

Minnetonka was a hidden lake. The Indians thought of it as a place of the spirit, a place blessed by God. They didn't mention the lake to the whites, purposely. In 1822 one of Colonel Snelling's sons paddled his way upstream from the Mississippi along Minnehaha Creek and came upon the lake at Gray's Bay. He was overwhelmed by it and didn't tell many others about it. Some officers from Fort Snelling also went over to the lake but did not tell anyone else about it.

In 1853 Governor Ramsey again followed the creek and "rediscovered" the lake, giving it its name. And then it became famous. In time great resort hotels were built around it, connected by "streetcar boats" peopled with Southerners escaping the summer heat. As the southern rivers were dammed and air conditioning was invented, the

---

*   See Index or Contents for separate article on this topic.

southern people could stay closer to home and the hotels burned or were torn down for other uses. Gradually it was surrounded with summer cottages and, after World War II, these were converted or replaced by all-year homes. So far there aren't many condominiums. The road system was never very good, nor can it ever be without destroying the beauty of the area: the roads are necessarily full of curves and turns as they meander among the bays.

Wayzata

Wayzata is a village of shops and brokerages and magnificent homes on the north shore of Lake Minnetonka about twelve miles due west of Minneapolis. Its name is pronounced "wuz-at'- uh." There are some who consider it the best address in the Twin Cities. Geographically it is quite small and only has a population of about three thousand. But a large area around it is within its postal area, enabling considerably more than three thousand people to say that they live in Wayzata. Since persons charged with unlawful conduct gave their addresses including Wayzata, when the number of criminals was divided by the actual population, Wayzata developed an unseemly high crime rate.

Every year the community celebrates James J. Hill Days and one wonders why. Mr. Hill was among the so-called robber barons who built America in the latter part of the nineteenth century. His relations with Wayzata were not such as to make him an object of reverence.

At one point, in 1867, the St. Paul & Pacific Railroad was clearing forests near Wayzata for its track west. Hill, who had no connection with the railroad, made a deal to buy all the trees that were being cut down for three dollars a cord. He then shipped it to St. Paul and sold it as firewood for nine dollars a cord. The farmers whose trees had been cut murmured a bit, but they did get their land cleared.

In 1878, because of bad management and a depression, the railroad was forced to sell, and Hill, who had started as a warehouse clerk, was able, with some friends, to buy it. In time he built a nice station in Wayzata which was heavily used by tourists in the summer, particularly Southerners with their slaves and horses. They would take the train to Wayzata and then go by boat to various summer resorts around this special lake. At one time seventeen opulent hotels and resorts existed. It even became a stop on Cook's Tours, as the Mall of America is today. It also attracted the weekend tourists from the surrounding area who could enjoy the boat trip on the lake.

But the bottom fell out of the tourist trade. Hotels burned down, boats sank, and the opulence that had been, was no longer.

Hill had put the railroad tracks along the lake, which was also right down the middle of Wayzata's main and only street, cutting off the only access to Minneapolis. Wayzata had become an incorporated city, and it sued Hill to move his tracks off the main street. The court ordered the city and the railroad to share the street, which angered Hill so much that he tore down its railroad station and built a new one a mile away, telling people if they wanted to have their main street, they'd have to walk an extra mile. Fifteen years later he relented and built the finest station on the line right where the original had been. It's now the headquarters for the Wayzata Historical Society and the Wayzata Chamber of Commerce. The double mainline tracks still run between the city and its lake, just as James J. Hill wanted.

The Warehouse District

There are over a dozen restaurants, maybe a dozen bars depending on how you classify things, about a half dozen theaters, several movie houses, a major league sports arena, some art galleries replete with artists, a whole bunch of shops, some yarn stores, and lots of small businesses.

It's not designed for haste or stress, though they are available. There are all kinds of people, of various colors, speaking several languages, holding different faiths or no faith, having different preferences, wearing styles ranging from grungy to conservative. They come from most every economic level. They're apt to be younger, maybe middle-aged.

In New York it might be Greenwich. In London it might be Soho. In Paris it might be the Left Bank or Montmartre. But the Warehouse District is different. It wasn't built for any of its present uses except maybe for a few sedate restaurants and saloons. It was built for warehousing everything necessary to supply a broad market of diverse people from frontiersmen to bankers. It was built of large brick buildings with high ceilings and huge wooden beams. The buildings carry the names of early, successful Minneapolis families: Butler, Wyman, Partridge, and Colwell. The latter building replaced an auctioning center which served the trappers and traders of fur, maybe the oldest form of masculine clothing and feminine enhancement.

For a time while the older uses were declining, there was much empty space, and the streets were dark and empty; even by daylight the pedestrians were scattered and hurried or were transported out of this world by the cheaper products of the grape and its cousins. But nature abhors a vacuum and so do city fathers and those pursuing the *nouveaux artes*. Artists liked the spacious lofts. The young found spaces for their pads and ateliers. Butler Square, a whole building, was converted to new uses by exposing and polishing its timbers and woodwork, attracting restaurants and boutiques. But it was lonely and ahead of its time. It was still off the beaten path. More restaurants crept in, appealing to various tastes, some attracting a lunch crowd from the office towers.

Then major league basketball needed a home, and Target*, a fabulous arena, was built at one end. More restaurants and shops followed. New streetlights put an end to the dark sidewalks. Huge parking ramps were built for this and the whole downtown work force. The interstate freeway system was connected, skyways were extended. The district became viable.

To the north, new buildings along the river became the Mississippi Mile*. The river's banks were recovered from industrial uses, a parkway was built. Walking paths and bike trails wound their way. Picnic areas were placed right next to the water. Warehouses overlooking the river were converted to condos and apartments.

The planners didn't plan, or they didn't seem to because they fitted their plans into the environment; they discovered what this constituency wanted and arranged it for them, without seeming to. It's easy to spend time there. It costs less than some other parts of town. It's an interesting mix of people.

The district is more or less bounded by Hennepin on the east, the freeway on the west, Eighth Street on the south, and the river on the north. It is still in metamorphosis. It makes a lot of people more contented with their lives, or for some, less discontented.

---

*   See Index or Contents for separate article on this topic.

Lowertown

If you like to walk, St. Paul's historic Lowertown was made for you. The landing on the Mississippi River became a major distribution center with warehouses serving much of the Upper Midwest. In 1983 the National Register of Historic Places put Lowertown on its list, protecting the area from demolition. Now a combination of residential and commercial uses makes this area a charming walk-about. You can get an excellent guide pamphlet from the St. Paul Heritage Preservation Commission at 25 West Fourth Street, St. Paul 55102

Start with the Union Station. Remember the glamor of the rails. Imagine all the travelers, freight, and mail that moved through this building which replaced one that burned in 1913. Airplanes can never achieve that feeling you got of being worldly and cosmopolitan as you strolled through the cars to the diner for a dinner on a white tablecloth with silver silverware, then to the bar car for a brandy before going back to your own private space to read or go to sleep between white sheets as the rails clickety-clacked beneath you, and you could peep out on a sleeping countryside whirling past. Think again of the hubbub of a depot, the conductors calling out the long list of towns and cities the train would serve. Alas, as with too many good things, in 1971 the station's use came to an end. Today the skylighted atrium exudes the aroma of restaurants. Gone are the laughter and excitement of family and friends meeting travelers.

On to the Railroad and Bank buildings. Here again, as so often in the Twin Cities, is the "Empire Builder," James J. Hill. He came from Rockland, Ontario in 1856 and became a warehouse clerk in Lowertown, developing into a successful businessman in his mid-forties and then buying and building the Great Northern, one of the nation's great railroads. For his holdings, he built what would remain the largest office building in the Twin Cities until the fifty-three-story IDS Tower was built in Minneapolis in 1956. But Hill's building remains, its atrium is now an indoor plaza. The railroad merged with the Burlington and the Northern Pacific to become the Burlington Northern and moved its headquarters to Texas.

Wandering on, you reach the Endicott Buildings built by Cass Gilbert, the architect of the state capitol and so many other buildings in the area. The Italian Renaissance buildings of red sandstone had many intricate designs that were unfortunately eroded by the sandblasting used to clean them.

The Pioneer Building used skyscraper construction for its twelve stories and contains the only open court still remaining.

In 1892 the Merchant's National Bank opened its doors with a two-story lobby. Its interesting red stone architecture was widely admired at the time. Plans to demolish it in 1967 were stymied by the National Registry.

Crossing to Mears Park, the Galtier Plaza looms into view. It was named after the priest who persuaded the powers that were to change the name of the city from Pigs Eye to St. Paul. Think of the renown if they hadn't changed it! The Galtier Plaza, often referred to as an urban village, combines retail shops, offices, and residential living. Terraces face onto the historic buildings surrounding the park.

Also viewed from Mears Park are the Noyes Brothers and Cutler Building, the Konantz Saddlery, and the Koehler and Hinrichs Company in the Stevens Building. The latter building was a wholesale house for butchers and meat packers. The saddlery began business in 1871 and in 1921 became a railroad printing house. The Noyes building housed importers and wholesale druggists with laboratories on the upper floors and clerks on the ground floor filling prescriptions from as far away as Montana. At one point in the

1970s, its small theater was used by Garrison Keillor's *Prairie Home Companion*.

On with the tour. The Walsh Block is typical of buildings put up with storefronts on the first floor and families utilizing the space above. Some of the buildings on south Seventh Street are interesting for their cast iron decorations, an inexpensive way to make the humble look elegant.

As you tour Lowertown you will note a certain similarity of the various buildings, caused by their use of the same materials such as brick from Lilydale and Chaska and stone from St. Cloud and Hinckley where one of the biggest fires in America occurred in 1917.

The First Baptist Church built its first chapel in 1851. Its present steeple proved too heavy for the swampy ground under the church, requiring extensive rebuilding in 1965. The Wacouta Street Warehouse, built by Cass Gilbert, demonstrates the intricate designs which made him famous. The first tenant, the Northwestern Paint Company, was most impressed by the cast iron columns and the fire-resistant timbers.

The Finch, Van Slyke, and McConville Drygoods Company built their building in 1911 for their wholesale dry goods business, using concrete slabs to support the heavy loads. Today they support 255 condominiums.

On the south side of Mears Park, the Powers Drygoods Company quickly became the major Twin Cities' department store and later built a building on Nicollet Avenue in Minneapolis. Subsequently they were bought by Federated Department Stores who sold them in turn to Donalsons, the area's second largest department store after Daytons. In time, Carson Pirie Scott of Chicago bought them, and they were subsequently bought by a Milwaukee retail chain. Daytons continues under the same local ownership and has grown into one of the four or five largest retailers in the country.

Farther along Fifth Street are two more of Cass Gilbert's buildings. They were built by Paul Gotzian, but the American House was renamed for its long-term tenant, the American Beauty Macaroni Company. In the 1980s it was renovated into residential use.

The 1905 St. Paul Rubber Company building was primarily used by the E.W. Honza's Printing Company's very heavy presses. In time rot and the weight of the presses made a major reconstruction necessary before the building could be converted to residential use.

When the Northern Pacific railroad was pushed through to the West Coast it became a major transporter of supplies, much originating in Duluth by transshipment from Great Lakes navigation. In 1907 it required a large headquarters building which was built at Prince and Broadway. Then in the recent past, the Northern Pacific merged with James J. Hill's Great Northern.

Today's visitors come by air and by freeway. They miss the colorful vista of the Lowertown buildings which greeted the visitors who came by paddlewheel up the river. The tour preserves it for those who will look.

Minnehaha

Where the Falls of Minnehaha
Flash and gleam among the oak trees,
Laugh and Leap into the valley,

Longfellow,
"Song of Hiawatha," 1855

It flows for twenty-two miles, from the Gray's Bay Dam at the eastern end of Lake Minnetonka through mostly parkland in the cities of Minnetonka, St. Louis Park, Edina, and Minneapolis, picking up water from the Chain of Lakes* to leap over a forty-foot falls and then through Minnehaha Park to the Mississippi nearby. It's not very big—maybe eight feet wide with the spring runoff. But with its ripples and little rapids it does seem to laugh.

It was the route that the first whites, maybe the first Indians, used to find Lake Minnetonka* from the Mississippi*. They both thought it and the lake too beautiful to share, so it was kept secret as long as possible. It was first called Falls Creek and then Brown's Creek. "Minnehaha" is much more glamorous and appropriate. It was used to power the saw mills and flour mills at Minnetonka and Edina*, but that service was cut off with the Gray's Bay Dam, which was put in to keep the waters of Lake Minnetonka at an even level.

Many people canoe from Minnetonka to the Mississippi every year. It requires quite a few portages over low highway bridges, and in dryer weather you may run aground occasionally. Or you could get stuck inside a culvert if the water is too high. But it's delightful. Have a friend meet you at the falls: it's a long way back.

The falls themselves are unusually beautiful, preserved in a large wooded park. Visiting dignitaries are usually taken to see them. In very dry seasons, a small hidden pump at the top of the falls is used for drinking if the dignitary is sufficiently important. At the rapids near the top of the falls, there is a life-size, bronze statue of Hiawatha carrying Minnehaha over the stream.

There is a large refectory near the falls, and picnic grounds so large that most of the Swedes of Minneapolis can fit in the space on Svenskarnasdag, their annual holiday.

---

*   See Index or Contents for separate article on this topic.

Below the falls there is a wide, woodsy trail meandering alongside the creek nearly a mile to the Mississippi. The steps down to the trail seem much steeper going up than they do going down.

Nordeast

Northeast from St. Anthony Falls with the river to its west is a district all its own. People brought up there feel nervous living in any other part of the area. It's a special place, heavily Eastern European ethnically but with a goodly mix of Germans and Scandinavians.

Its main street is Central Avenue which runs from the Third Avenue Bridge up to Columbia Heights, a long commercial strip, starting with the Godfrey House* and the Central Labor Union's headquarters, past car dealers, housing for the elderly, across railroad tracks, near the School Board headquarters, near the Firefighters Museum*, with every kind of merchandise and service that could be needed.

It seems to keep to itself. It has its own bars and saloons and several excellent restaurants which attract outsiders. It has its own churches, many of them slightly forbidding on the exterior, like pictures of churches in Poland and the Ukraine, but warm on the inside, with that special emotional music, the intense liturgy, and incense. There is noth-

---

*   See Index or Contents for separate article on this topic.

ing like it in the rest of the city except the Greek Orthodox Church on the east side of Calhoun, which is also warmly beautiful on the outside.

More so possibly than the rest of the cities, the people here seem quite content with each other and with their families and their neighborhoods. They have all that they need, why go elsewhere?

Camp Snoopy

Everything a child could want to do or see or taste or hear or touch or smell—or ride on. There are twenty rides, ten eateries, seven shops, five attractions, and four stages. You can go into a mine and pan for real gold. You can buckle into a two-seated gondola and be turned every which way including up. You can ride a hollowed log down a mountain chute amidst lots of moving figures and then suddenly go over a forty-foot waterfall. You can eat a cake made of sweet confections with fruit toppings and powdered sugar, or just ice cream or cotton candy. You can play in an arcade with over a hundred token-operated games. The family can sit down to a Bavarian Oktoberfest all year around, with German entertainment and some beer or wine. You can climb into a bump-into-each-other car in an old-fashioned amusement park. There is a long, mountainous roller coaster or a "ride" in the middle of a movie adventure of non-stop suspense. Kids can play in a room full of endless boxes of building blocks. You can get all the goodies you have come to expect from Knott's Berry Market. You can listen to country or bluegrass to your heart's content. It goes on and on.

It's Knott's Camp Snoopy, an amusement park about a block long and half a block wide, completely covered by a ceiling way up there, cool in the summer, warm in the winter, right in the middle of the Mall of America. You buy a card when you enter for whatever you want to spend, or whatever your kids plead for, and then you swipe it through a reader.

You're surrounded by a thick layer of department stores, boutiques, restaurants, shops, movies, and whatever. The four corners have Nordstroms, Macys, Bloomingdales, and Sears. There are maybe five hundred shops! It would take you all day just to count them. On each end there is a free covered, multilevel parking ramp for thousands of cars, divided into fourteen sections for easier identification. Bus lines come inside, right up to the doors. Freeways swirl around. Over a million people come to visit, many, maybe most, of them from outside the Twin Cities. Northwest Airlines provides bargain rates. Travel agencies from all over the world include it on tours. People drive from all over to spend days in it.

It's the *Mall of America,* nicknamed the Megamall. It's the largest shopping mall in the United States, the second largest in the world. It's massive. It's clean. It's efficient. And it's fun.

The Chain of Lakes

There are five clear blue lakes in a row along the west side of Minneapolis: Brownie Lake, Cedar Lake, Lake of the Isles, Lake Calhoun, and Lake Harriet. Some people make it six by counting Lake Nokomis, but it is several miles downstream on Minnehaha Creek. Cedar Lake was originally given the name Lake Leavenworth. Lake Harriet was named for the wife of Colonel Leavenworth. Lake Calhoun was named for the southern statesman. They were carved out by a glacier ten to twelve thousand years ago and filled with the water of the melting glacier. They have clay-lined bottoms which hold the water. They have received sand and rotting vegetable matter through the ages to give them a fertile coating for the plant life necessary for the fish. They are said to be excellent fishing lakes, if only because there are so many sailboats and canoes that no one ever fishes them.

The lakes are heavily used. There are paths for bikers and separate one-way paths for skaters and pedestrians. The geese use all the paths, as is obvious. There are swimming beaches on Cedar, Calhoun, and Harriet; Isles has a muddy bottom and Brownie is too small and isolated. They have been carefully zoned: there are only two high-rises, both on the northwest corner of Calhoun. The lakes are owned by the Park Department, including the land and the parkways around all of them.

Before the Europeans, the area was sparsely occupied by the Dakotas, specifically the Medawakantanwan tribe whose territories were Kaposia, Black Dog's, Chaska's, and Shakopee's. Kaposia has disappeared. Black Dog's has been preserved as part of the Minnesota Valley Wildlife Center* and also as the site for a major generating plant along the Minnesota River. Chaska and Shakopee are thriving small cities along the river in Scott and Carver counties. Shakopee is the site for Murphy's Landing*, an Indian casino, Valley Fair Amusement Park, and a temporarily closed horse racing track.

---

*   See Index or Contents for separate article on this topic.

When they lived by the lakes, the Indians lived on corn and vegetables and hunting. By 1800 they had become used to the white traders and their products. In 1819 a remarkable man named Taliaferro became the Indian Agent located at Fort Snelling. He was persuaded that the Indians could not long survive by hunting and fur trading, and he worked assiduously to convert them to farming. To help them and protect them, he persuaded Cloudman, an Indian, to create a village which he called Eatonville on the southeast side of Lake Calhoun, near Lake Harriet. By 1831 about 300 Indians had settled in the town and joined each other in farming. Samuel and Gideon Pond, unordained missionaries, joined them and built a 12-by-16-foot log cabin on the north shore.

But then in 1839 Chief Hole-in-the-Day, an Ojibwe chief from up in Anoka about twenty-five miles to the north, raided the farming settlement, killing Cloudman's son-in-law. War parties were organized and battles took place on the Rum River and the St. Croix River. Over seventy-five Ojibwas were killed with only fifteen Medawakantanwan lost. The seventy-five scalps were brought back to Lake Calhoun and an all-night scalp dance was held by the whole village. The missionary Ponds watched part of it and described it as hellish and depraved.

The Indians moved west, and in 1845 the land was opened to the Europeans. Mostly, though, the Europeans preferred to settle by the built-up area around St. Anthony Falls. The first European to build a home was Charles Mosseaux in 1849, on the east side of Calhoun. In 1857 there were 200 settlers, by 1859, 2,000. In 1879 Mosseaux sold his property to William King who acquired the land which is now between Lyndale, named for his father, the Rev. Lyndon King, and Berry Parkway between Lake Calhoun and Lake Harriet. He built the extensive Lyndale Farmstead at Thirty-eighth and renamed ten blocks of Dupont Avenue, King's Highway, later turning the farmstead over to the

Park Board which retains parts of it today as their maintenance area. Mr. King also gave the land for the Rock Garden* and the Rose Garden* and the Bird Sanctuary* along the north side of Lake Harriet and developed Lakewood Cemetery along the rolling woods on the southwest side of Lake Calhoun.

By 1880 there was a boom in lakeside resorts, and some large properties were built on both sides of Lake Calhoun, one on the east side now replaced with a gorgeous Greek Orthodox Church. The Minneapolis & St. Louis Railway ran a line out to serve the area. In 1899 Minikahda Country Club built its magnificent clubhouse for $15,000 alongside its golf course on the west side of Calhoun with a large boathouse down on the water's edge. The lakes were heavily used for sailing and swimming in the summer and for trotting races over the ice in the winter. Dan Patch, who set world trotting records and who was once owned by Fish Jones*, raced on Calhoun.

Along the north side of Lake Calhoun and the south side of Cedar Lake the predominant buildings were ice houses, great ugly windowless sheds where the blocks of ice cut from the lakes were stored in layers with sawdust between the layers to keep the ice from freezing into one huge block. During the summer months, these blocks were carried over the whole city every day in horse-drawn wagons and sold to housewives who put signs in their windows showing how many pounds they wanted for their refrigerators. Little boys chipped off bits of ice to suck on. In the winter, the horses provided the cores to deadly snowballs.

As with any lake, the shoreline vegetation of the Chain of Lakes encroached on the water, weeds gradually moving in, followed by other vegetation until the shore became a

---

*   See Index or Contents for separate article on this topic.

bog. If left alone, the bog would take over the entire lake, and gradually the water would recede and a new lowland would be formed. To prevent this, in 1909 Lake of the Isles was dredged, including a channel to Calhoun. In 1911 and 1915 Calhoun was dredged, with the fill being used on the south side to create new land for homes.

After a severe rainstorm in 1951, many basements in this new land were flooded. The residents wanted storm drains put down their streets to take off future rains. The city engineer pointed out that their basement floors were below the lake's waterline so that any storm drains would move water into their basements, not out.

Today's fashionable Lowry Hill was known as "The Devil's Backbone." Tom Lowry changed the name when he platted Kenwood* as a luxury area where houses were required to cost at least $3,000. A railroad station was built at Twenty-first Street and mansions followed, many still carefully preserved as galleries and residences. A characteristic of the neighborhood was not only these sumptuous homes but the huge woodpile beside each for heat in the winter. The area was completed by the Peavey Fountain at the north end of Lake of the Isles, a marble basin with a marble obelisk in the center, basically designed as a watering place for horses.

On the southeast corner of Lake Calhoun is an archery range used both by individuals and contests.

There is seepage under the area between Lake Harriet and Lake Calhoun to allow drainage into Lake Harriet for the upper lakes. It was developed into the wooded William Berry Park. At the Lake Harriet end, there was a pump used by the neighborhood for fresh water. It is still used today, with cars lined up almost every evening. There was also a

---

*   See Index or Contents for separate article on this topic.

bandstand—several as the years went by, each more elegant than its predecessor. Concerts were, and are, played every summer evening with an audience sitting in cars, on park benches, lying on the grass, or in boats floating quietly in the lake. On the west side of Lake Harriet, up on the hillside, is a little park with the charming name of Beard's Plaisance. An outlet on the southeast side connects Lake Harriet to Minnehaha Creek and thence to the Mississippi with park land on both sides.

Crocus Hill

It was a little place, but now it's bigger—or maybe it isn't. Street numbers change with abandon. Street names have a confusing similarity, like Boston suburbs that take a root name for one town and then create new towns with the same root and four or five prefixes or suffixes. It was, maybe is, a sought-after address.

Crocus Hill was named by an early settler for the profusion of the beautiful flowers that grew there. It's on a knob of a hill just below Summit Avenue near the University Club. Louis Hill, son of James J. Hill, was an early builder. Others came with Victorian homes that are comfortably large without being mansions.

A house may have an address on Crocus Hill though its main entrance is on Fairmont. But if it changes to the Fairmont address it may disappear into another mailing route where it may not be found. Or a house may be at #10 Crocus Hill but its next door neighbor is #10 Goodrich. Mail carriers make a career out of it.

It was small, three or four blocks, so it got itself combined into the next district and got stretched way to Lexington. The city calls it by its new name, but Realtors much prefer to call the whole thing Crocus Hill. The houses are carefully maintained. Several have been purchased by younger people who have restored anything that needed to be restored.

Whatever its name, it's a delightful place to live.

The University of Minnesota

The university is universal. There are the colleges, of course, in most every professional specialty and liberal arts. Many of them have high national reputations: the law school; the school for mortuary sciences; the medical complex with its hospital, its schools of medicine, public health, ophthalmology, dentistry, and human genetics. There is the Hubert Humphrey Institute for advanced study, General College for those who need the fundamentals, and on and on. It has some 45,000 students plus faculty, plus administration, plus maintenance.

There are also athletics of every known variety with new ones being improvised daily by ingenious students. There are "Big Ten" sports for both men and women, there are intramural sports for both men and women, and there are sedentary sports, chess for instance, for men and women. In 1995 it hosted the "Final Four" of women's basketball.

Scattered through the buildings are galleries, libraries, laboratories, displays, and wall hangings, making it interesting to wander into the buildings, if security permits, just to see what the particular specialty has displayed for you.

And there are places that will accept your money: movies and theaters, restaurants and bars, clothiers new and used, video and audio in all their permutations, books of all types and prices and ages. The stores are pretty much concentrated in "Dinkytown" (derivation defies investigation), on the "West Bank" (along Cedar and Riverside), and along Washington on the east bank.

Excelsior

The founders of Excelsior must have been moved by inspiration and hope to have named their community after a word that means "higher" and is used in contexts similar to its sibling "excelsus," meaning "highest," pretty much reserved for descriptions of the deity. The optional meaning of excelsior is unacceptable, meaning finely shredded wood used to start fires. The community would not do that.

Excelsior has been around for a long time in the brief history of the Twin Cities. It was the first town on Lake Minnetonka, and some of its first buildings are still there, carefully preserved and in use. Its main avenue, Water Street, speaks almost of another age. The shops along it have kept their old store fronts but have modernized their insides to provide most anything a contemporary person could want. It gives an impression of a restored city but it isn't: it never deteriorated so it's never needed restoration. It was on the early railroads and was a terminus of the streetcar network and thus a port for the streetcar boats which were built to resemble the streetcars of the Twin City Rapid Transit Company. The boats plied the waters of the lake, calling at many ports. They were a necessity for some resorts and a pleasure for a Sunday's activity. The boats lost too many passengers when the network of roads was built. Most of them burned. One sank and has lately been raised and is being lovingly restored by volunteers.

Excelsior had a magnificent amusement park with thrill rides and rifle shoots. There was a rumor that its roller coaster had been condemned as unsafe, but the rumor was untrue and served only to give the riders a bigger thrill. It had a huge dance hall, which was very popular on weekends, a swimming beach, and a marina. It was a well-equipped lake village and still is. And it has inspirational churches, new and old.

Excelsior has indeed moved higher: it serves a large and populous area of upscale and middle-class homes. Its amusement park and marina have given way to lakeside condominiums and restaurants; its dance hall has become doctors' offices. Swimming beaches have given way to sanitized pools. The Old Log Theater* on the outskirts gives it continuing culture. The streetcar* boats are long gone, but the lake is dotted with sailboats and churned by cruisers, livelier than ever. The restored streetcar boat may return one of these years.

Kenwood

It settled early, from the southern edge of Loring Park to the south shore of Lake of the Isles. Mansions grew west along Mount Curve Avenue on the brow of Lowry Hill and east along Groveland. It spread south along the easy curves of Kenwood Parkway, from the railroad tracks on the west to Hennepin Avenue on the east, to Lake Street on the south. Besides Lake of the Isles and adjacent Kenwood Park, it has acquired other anchors. The Guthrie* and Walker Art

---

*   See Index or Contents for separate article on this topic.

Center* and Sculpture Garden* have come to the northeast, across from Loring Park and the Parade Ground, in sight of the Basilica* and near to the Episcopal Cathedral of St Mark and the Hennepin Avenue Methodist Church*. On the south it is based on Uptown* and the northern shores of Lake Calhoun. It has achieved some national fame for the house where Mary Tyler Moore lived in her television years.

It is an area of fine old homes, some a century or more old. They were built by the well-to-do of the old families. Often three generations lived in a house, with servant girls in the attic or the carriage house. Originally, of course, transportation was all dependent on the horse. The Peaveys, who contributed much to the parks and well-being of the city, built a fine fountain and watering place for horses where Kenwood Parkway flows into Lake of the Isles Boulevard. As is all of Kenwood, it is old, stately, and maintained.

Gradually the older families died out or moved to other sections. Some of the houses became genteel rooming houses or were partitioned into apartments. But they were maintained and their yards were kept up. Kenwood has always been a good address.

Now it has been regentrified. Many of the rooming houses and partitioned homes have been restored to single-family dwellings. A few homes have been torn down, but they have been replaced with excellent moderns that fit well into the environment. It's become an even better address because it's close to downtown, near the lakes with their walking and biking paths, churches of all faiths, a large and verdant park. The railroad yards with their noise and soot are gone; a racial mix has grown approximating the city's.

---

*   See Index or Contents for separate article on this topic.

White Bear Lake

The town of White Bear Lake was founded in 1858, the same year Minnesota was admitted to the Union as the thirty-second state. Perched beside White Bear Lake, which Mark Twain described as "A Lovely Sheet of Water," it quickly developed as a resort town favored, after the Civil War, by Easterners and later Southerners anxious to escape the heat and noise of the cities. To show off the history of the area and the legends of the Dakotas and the Ojibwas, several walking trails have been developed.

You will see a bookstore, originally the White Bear House. Nearby is a barbershop. In its previous days as a part of a bank, it was the scene of a bank robbery in which the robber got $500 and tried to jump onto a moving train, missed, was chased, and eventually was shot dead along with a private citizen.

At the Railroad Park you can recall the heydays when it required fourteen tracks to accommodate all the people who came up from St. Paul. It cost fifty cents and took twenty minutes, a considerable improvement over the pre-1868 days of horse and buggy which required three hours.

Down the street is an Italianate-inspired store front built in 1886 for a meat market. Next to it is a Beaux Arte style building from the prosperous twenties.

The first general store was built in 1871 near the depot by Daniel Getty, whose second store is still in use. The first schoolhouse, twenty feet square, was built in 1857 of tamarack logs, using animal skins to keep out January's cold.

Farther along is one of White Bear Lake's treasures: the Fillebrown House, built in 1879 and recognized by the National Historic Register. Now restored to its original style by the White Bear Area Historical Society, it was affectionately known as the "Red Chalet" because of the tearoom opened in the Depression. It was originally built as a summer cottage. In addition to the tearoom, it has been used as a nursery school, a music studio, and a private residence. Another house on the National Registry is the Cobb House, built by one of the area's first settlers.

With many visitors, there were many hotels, usually built as mansions with all the conveniences. The Chateaugay had a telephone! Most have since burned down. If you could not afford one of these grand hotels, there were white tents as an alternative. The fabulous Wildewood Amusement Park attracted thrill-seekers with its roller coaster and its huge, 100-foot water slide plus the usual attractions.

Mark Twain mentions White Bear Lake in *Life on the Mississippi*, referring to its great healing powers and spreading its name and reputation. People did feel better after being there. Besides Mark Twain, other notables were Zelda and F. Scott Fitzgerald, and the Prohibition Era gangsters Ma Barker, Baby Face Nelson, and John Dillinger, who were reputed to have hideouts somewhere in the area.

A path leads to an island named Manitou, the Indians' "Great Spirit" who is also embodied in a white bear. Legend says an Ojibwa maiden and a Dakota brave were fighting for their lives with a bear. Some say the brave killed the bear, some say the lovers died together.

One of the few Civil War monuments in Minnesota was built in 1913 to honor the thirty-five citizens who fought in that war. The lack of monuments is odd considering that the Minnesota regiment is credited with saving the first day of Gettysburg for the Union, losing almost half its strength, this from a state which then had only about 50,000 residents.

Indians buried their dead along the lakeshore, covering them with black dirt from which lush vegetation grew. The graves were transferred to the cemetery in 1889 and a monument was erected to remember them.

There are brochures for these walking tours at the Historical Society.

Hours: Fillebrown House: 1:00-4:00 Sundays, June-September **Phone**: 426-0479
Parking: Nearby **Admission**: Adults $2; children under 13 $1 **Address**: White Bear Area Historical Society, 4735 Lake Avenue, White Bear Lake, 55110

Frogtown

The railroads needed men, lots of men, to help them span half a continent. And the men came—mostly French Canadians—and settled their families near the first depot, just north of St. Paul's business center where the Capitol is, and spread west to the railroad area now known as Bandana Square. It stretched itself between Dale and Snelling and north of University Avenue, the major inner-city thoroughfare until Interstate 94 was built.

The origin of its peculiar name is in some doubt. Some say that the area was swampy, a fertile habitat for frogs. Others say that the French had acquired the nickname of "frog" from their nasal accent so that "Frogtown" was applied to the area where they settled. It's a distinctive name for an area that has been able to become and remain distinctive.

The Saint Croix River

It rises in northwestern Wisconsin about twenty-five miles south of Lake Superior, so close that there have been suggestions to use it and the Brule River to dig a canal from the lake to the Mississippi; but any commercial value would surely be greatly outweighed by the huge damage to the thick and wild forest land that would be ravaged.

It quickly becomes the boundary between Minnesota and Wisconsin for 130 miles until it flows into the Mississippi at Hastings in the southeastern corner of the Metro area. During its last thirty miles, south from Stillwater in the northeastern corner, its character changes from a woodland stream to a stately river flowing between high forested banks, reminiscent of the Hudson River above New York.

It was the reason for the early settlement of Stillwater and its growth until it almost became the state capital. The immigrants, particularly the Scandinavians, went by riverboat up the Mississippi, then branched off to the St. Croix to Stillwater, the head of its navigation, and thence to settle nearby at Scandia*, a journey that has been much written about and made several times into a movie. Commerce followed, carrying supplies to the new territory before land transportation was feasible.

It remains a treasure today. Houses and marinas and some villages have been built on it, mostly with careful regard for the unparalleled scenery. You could take your boat from the St. Croix up the Mississippi to St. Paul or Minneapolis, or downstream to New Orleans, or by the Ohio to Cincinnati or Pittsburgh. But they would be long trips. On a Sunday afternoon in summer, it is covered with boats,

---

* See Index or Contents for separate article on this topic.

basking in beauty a few miles from the heart of St. Paul, part of this wonderful land of water.

Uptown

It's not a mall, but it has a mall. It's not an entertainment center, but it has movies, theaters, video machines, and at least twenty restaurants. It's not commercial, being in the middle of an upscale residential area near a lake, but it has lawyers, doctors, bankers, brokers, printers, jewelers, clothiers, cosmeticians, grocers, butchers, and cobblers. There are book stores, music stores, drug stores, a condom store, framing stores, sports stores, card shops, and shops with miscellaneous and exotic wares and services. And there are three schools and two churches.

"Uptown," how do you describe it? During the Depression years, Morris & Christie had exotic and simple foods, and the fresh produce was displayed on the sidewalk; Bonhus Hardware supplied everything needed to keep a house functioning; the World Theater had moving clouds in its ceiling, and the Uptown Theater had Bank Nights. Walgreen's Drugstore was almost a department store and had bargain prices. It served the salutary function of providing an oasis of heat for high school kids walking a mile or more to school and home for lunch in these pre-bus, pre-lunchroom days. The Rainbow Cafe was an elegant restaurant; there was a Chinese restaurant before such were common, and a great ice cream store, the Hasty Tasty. During the war, Morris & Christie would save bananas and Jell-O for its good customers. Though it has changed, it is still a wonderful neighborhood area.

Today it is much bigger, much more diverse, much busier, more eclectic, noisier. There are lots of national franchise outlets and lots of parking lots, and great opportunities for people-watching. The people now are younger, more conscious of being watched, but there are still the kids and the older, longtime residents. There is a huge art fair in the late summer with thousands of people amid hundreds of displays of paintings, crafts, whatever. Cars are detoured for blocks. Most everybody is smiling and being "Minnesota Nice" to each other.

This is "Uptown," a pulsing, liberal neighborhood. It's actually southwest of downtown, near the northeast corner of Lake Calhoun and the southeast corner of Lake of the Isles, at Hennepin Avenue and Lake Street, which is the same as Thirtieth Street, in Minneapolis 55408. As it says of itself, it is "South of Downtown, Left of Center."

Historic Houses

Burwell House

The Ojibwa and Dakota Indians were the first proven permanent settlers in Minnetonka, though they believed that it had once been inhabited by a race which became extinct before they arrived, and historians think there were two groups ahead of them: one which died off because the mammoths disappeared, the other which just disappeared a century or so before the Dakotas and Ojibwa came. The first Europeans to visit the area where the Burwell House now stands came from Fort Snelling in 1922 up Minnehaha Creek, which was earlier known as Brown's Creek or Falls Creek. Thirty years later a claim was staked where McGinty Road crossed the creek and the first sawmill in Minnesota west of the Mississippi was built to process the area's thick woods of oak, maple, elm, red cedar, and basswood.

Photo courtesy of the City of Minnetonka Historical Society

A settlement grew up around the sawmill: a furniture factory and a paint and varnish shop. The sawmill supplied the oak timbers needed for the suspension bridge, which was the first bridge anywhere to span the Mississippi*. The sawmill closed in 1860, but in 1869 a flour mill was opened and Charles Burwell became its manager. In 1873, at a cost of $3,250, he built a charming Italianate house. His wife had died the same year but he and his two children lived in the house with his parents, brother, and sister. In 1876 he remarried and had two more children.

Later a kitchen was added and an enlarged porch. After the mill was closed, its office building was moved near the house to serve as a garage. Some of the mill workers' cottages also were moved for quarters for Mr. Burwell's mother. In 1914 extensive remodeling was done to modern-

---

*   See Index or Contents for separate article on this topic.

ize the house, most of which has now been undone to restore it to its 1883 condition.

The first floor consists of a kitchen, dining room, parlor, and the parents' bedroom. Upstairs the back bedroom was used by the hired help. There are three family bedrooms and a bathroom which had a tub and washstand. The privy was out back in the woodshed, and a back stairway assisted in a more rapid and private access. The tower room served as a playroom for the children.

Hours: Thursday and Friday 10:00-4:30; First and third Saturday 10:00-3:00 **Phone**: 939-8200 **Parking**: Adequate nearby **Admission**: Free **Address**: McGinty Rd. and County Road #5 [Minnetonka Blvd.] Mailing address: 14600 Minnetonka Blvd., Minnetonka 55345

The James J. Hill Mansion

Illustration courtesy of the James J. Hill House

In the nineteenth century, a century of rugged individualists, James J. Hill stood out as truly a man among men. After twenty years working his way up in the profitable freight business, with four others in 1878 he purchased the nearly bankrupt St. Paul and Pacific Railroad. Sixteen years later, by 1893, the railroad had pushed all the way to Puget Sound. Mr. Hill is reputed to have said, "Give me a batch of Swedes and a batch of whisky and I'll build a railroad to hell." In 1890 he changed the name to Great Northern and it grew strong with the best locomotives, grades, tracks, and lowest prices.

With this background, it is no surprise that the mansion he built was a reflection of his own rugged personality. The house was built to suit him. The project was personally supervised by him as though he were building the Great Northern railroad itself. Construction was begun in 1888 and completed in 1891 at a cost of $522,854.38. After including the prices of custom interior decorations, landscaping, gatehouse, barn, power plant, and mushroom cave, the final cost was almost a million dollars—in 1890 dollars.

The mansion that Mary and James Hill lived in with their eight children had 36,000 square feet! The exterior was made of red and brown sandstone imported from Massachusetts. The roof was slate sent to Minnesota from Maine. The children must have had fun playing hide and seek in the thirty-two rooms. And with thirteen bathrooms, there was never a wait.

The basement floor included the kitchen, the laundry and drying room, the servants' dining room and hall, storerooms, cellar, boiling room, and a wine cellar.

The first floor had the drawing room, breakfast room, dining room, music room, reception room, library, and various terraces. Here, too, was the lovely skylighted gallery, home of the Hills' collection of the Barbizon School of Painting. The second floor had rooms for the parents, their five daughters, and their guests. The third floor was for the three sons, the servants, a gymnasium, and sewing facilities—a home to be enjoyed. It was rumored that once 2,000 guests were assembled, but because of all the rooms, the count was uncertain.

The mansion was occupied until 1925 by the Hill family. It was home to the Archdiocese of St. Paul from 1925 to 1978, when it was purchased by the Minnesota Historical Society, with funds from the Legislature. The Society is treasuring this significant bit of the past and preserving it for the future.

Hours: Open for guided tours Wednesday-Saturday **Phone**: 297-2555 **Parking**: Curbside **Admission**: Over 15: $3, 6-15: $1, under 6 free. **Address**: 240 Summit Avenue, St. Paul 55102

Godfrey House

The year was 1847 when Ard Godfrey arrived in St. Anthony to build a dam and a sawmill on the Mississippi River* at St. Anthony Falls, leaving behind his family in Orono, Maine. The dam and mill were completed in 1848, and at the same time he commenced building a home for his family. He returned to Maine for them. On the trip west, they stopped in Beloit, Wisconsin, to visit family. With winter setting in, Harriet Godfrey, now pregnant, remained there with her sister-in-law while Ard returned to St. Anthony. Harriet and the children arrived at their new home in the spring of 1849 and a baby girl was born. Little Harriet became the first white child of American descent to be born in St. Anthony. She was one of ten Godfrey children.

---

*   See Index or Contents for separate article on this topic.

Ard Godfrey House
Old St. Anthony
Minneapolis

Illustration courtesy of the Ard Godfrey House

The Godfreys lived in the house until 1852, when Ard built a larger home. In 1905 the first house was sold to the Minnesota Territorial Association and moved to Chute Square. Later it was taken over by the Minneapolis Park Board, which used it as a museum until 1934 when it was closed and boarded up due to the lack of funds. The same year it was declared a historical building.

In 1976, needing a way to celebrate the Bicentennial, The Woman's Club of Minneapolis undertook to restore the lovely, boarded-up old home and present it to the city as a present. After considerable discussion, in April 1976 the Park Board leased the building to the club without rent.

It was a difficult labor as each bit of work had to be meticulously studied for historical accuracy. Volunteers spent thousands of hours researching and scrubbing. The Minneapolis Building and Construction Trades Council, kitty-corner neighbors, were so impressed by the ladies' enthusiasm that bricklayers, carpenters, and sheet metal workers donated their time and money to help complete the work, with help from another neighbor, Boisclair Corporation.

The home was furnished with exact period accuracy. Each piece of furniture, each picture, the clock on the wall, the cradle where little Harriet slept, the wood stove, the piano, each bit of miscellany fits the house as the Godfreys knew it in the days before Minneapolis even had a name.

It continues to be maintained for the Park Board by the Woman's Club, which staffs it with volunteers for public tours every summer.

Hours: Friday-Monday noon-3:30 June-September **Parking**: Curbside **Admission**: Adults $1.00, seniors 50¢, students 6-18 25¢ **Address**: Central and University Avenues **Phone**: 870-8001. Minneapolis Inquiries to The Woman's Club, 410 Oak Grove, Minneapolis 55403

Sibley and Faribault Houses

The following is from a brochure published by the Sibley House Association:

Turn back the hands of time to the early 19th century. It was a time of fur trading, the frontier days of early dealings with the American Indians." Only a few thousand people lived in the whole state of Minnesota, probably less than half of them near Fort Snelling.

It was 1835, and Henry Hastings Sibley came to this area as a representative of the American Fur Company. He built his house across the river from Fort Snelling, and set up trade with Indians of the Dakota and Ojibwa tribes.

Photo courtesy of the Sibley House Association

This early contact between Euro-Americans and American Indians began a cultural exchange that was to shape the history of our country. The Sibley Historic Site now houses one of the largest collections of 19th-century Dakota and Ojibwa artifacts (over 20,000 items), including ceremonial pipes, quilts, and manuscripts.

Henry Sibley was instrumental in the earliest history of the state of Minnesota. Active in public affairs, Sibley served as a justice of the peace, postmaster, Territorial Delegate to Congress, and in 1858, when Minnesota became a state, he was elected its first governor. He had married Sarah Jane Steele (sister of Franklin Steele, one-time owner of Fort Snelling), and together they entertained a stream of visitors and politicians through the Sibley House and other local structures.

The history of the site is unique in its development and change over the years. In 1862, when the Sibleys moved out to live in St. Paul, the house was used as a school run by the Sisters of St. Joseph. It was later used as an artist's studio and school, a warehouse, and eventually abandoned with much of its interior destroyed by transients.

In 1910 the Sibley House Association was established to help preserve the houses and buildings on the site. The Minnesota Society of the Daughters of the American Revolution [DAR] obtained the Sibley House from the Parish of St. Peter, Mendota, Minnesota. For over 80 years the DAR and its affiliated organization, the SHA, have operated the site, keeping the house and its properties open to the public.

Photo courtesy of the Sibley House Association

In 1837, Jean Baptiste Faribault, a colleague of Sibley's, replaced an earlier log dwelling built on the site in 1826 with a house made of limestone. As part of the historic site, the Faribault House contains a large part of the Bishop Henry Whipple Collection (primarily Minnesota Indian artifacts). This is one of the top ten Native American Indian collections in the United States.

Hours: Tuesday-Saturday 10:00-5:00, Sunday 12:00-5:00 May-October. Tours on the hour **Phone**: 452-1596 **Parking**: Ample **Admission:** Adults $3.00, seniors $2.50, children 6-16 $1.00 **Address**: 55 D Street, Mendota 55150 (a mile north of the east end of the Mendota Bridge, across from Ft. Snelling)

Alexander Ramsey House

In 1849 thirty-four-year-old Pennsylvanian Alexander Ramsey made the arduous trip to the newly emerging Territory of Minnesota. He became the first territorial governor, and in the next thirty years he played a dominant role in Minnesota politics. He was the state's second governor, served two years in the United States Senate, and was appointed Secretary of War by President Hayes.

Photo courtesy of the Alexander Ramsey House

His wife, Anna, an educated wealthy Pennsylvanian, accompanied him to the frontier where she suffered the loss of two sons and deterioration of her own health. She was nevertheless a strong leader in the social and cultural world of the new territory. All people, regardless of race and diverse background, were welcomed and enjoyed her hospitality.

The Victorian mansion was completed in 1872, twenty-three years after their arrival in Minnesota. Small in comparison with the James J. Hill house* up on the hill less than a mile away, the three-story house is currently furnished as it was over a century ago. It consists of fifteen rooms with black walnut, hand-carved woodwork. There are marble fireplaces, crystal chandeliers, and a valuable collection of china and crystal glassware collected by the Ramseys. Of note, too, is a dollhouse made for Laura Furness, their granddaughter.

---

*　See Index or Contents for separate article on this topic.

Photo courtesy of the Alexander Ramsey House

The kitchen has been restored and many of Anna Ramsey's recipes are used in preparing pastries, breads, and other foods. Guides in period costumes tell the story of the life and hardships of the Ramsey's frontier life.

The mansion was willed to the state of Minnesota in 1964 and is managed by the Minnesota Historical Society. Tours begin in a reconstructed carriage house where visitors will find a wide array of Victorian items in the Museum Shop.

Hours: April to Thanksgiving, Tuesday-Saturday 10:00-3:00. Available by reservation until January 1st. **Phone**: 296-8760 **Parking**: Curbside **Admission**: Adults $3, children 6-15 $2 **Address**: 265 S. Exchange, St. Paul 55102 (one block south of West 7th Street on Walnut St. to Exchange St.)

Stevens House

Built in 1850, the John H. Stevens House was the first permanent settler's home in what is now Minneapolis. Col. Stevens and his wife made the home a social and civic hub of the city, though it was as yet a mere village. Many people met here, and discussions were lively concerning schools, government, and a name for the place.

Photo courtesy of the John H. Stevens House

Originally the home was on the riverbank, under the protection of Fort Snelling. However, in 1896 seven thousand school children participated in relays to tug the house to its present site abutting Minnehaha Park*.

The house was closed and boarded up at the turn of the century. Then in 1980 the Junior League of Minneapolis took as its project the restoration of the Stevens House to its original appearance. Finished in 1986, the house now serves as an interpretive history center managed by a community based board of directors with various programs for the public throughout the year focusing on early Minneapolis history based on photographs, artifacts, and visual and audio presentations. Staff and docents are available to help.

Hours: Summer: Tuesday-Friday 1:00-4:00; Saturday and Sunday 12:30-5:00. September: Saturday and Sunday 12:30-3:00. Other months by appointment **Phone**: 722-2220 **Parking**: Nearby **Admission**: Adults $1.00, students 25¢ **Address**: 4901 Minnehaha Avenue, Minneapolis 55417 (just south of Minnehaha Parkway at the east edge of Minnehaha Park)

---

*   See Index or Contents for separate article on this topic.

Outdoor Activities

The Minnesota Zephyr

Remember Milwaukee's "Hiawatha," the Northwestern's "400," and the Burlington's "Zephyr"? They all went from Minneapolis to Chicago in 400 minutes, a mile a minute, and in the height of luxury, sleek, beautiful, a little bit tipsy, the rails clicking a background rhythm. We knew we had the best trains in the country. One of them is back! The "Zephyr" is all aluminum, just like its predecessor, its engine the same dominating, blunt red-striped blue monster, its seats with the same wide view of the countryside, its food maybe even better.

It doesn't go a mile a minute, but then, with such beautiful countryside to travel, slowness is better. A leisurely meal through lush fields on tracks first laid in the 1870s takes you seven miles paralleling the St. Croix River then turning west through Dutchtown, along Brown's Creek, climbing 250 feet at a 2.2 percent grade, past the Oak Glen Country Club to Duluth Junction where it pauses and returns to the restored Depot at Stillwater*.

---

* See Index or Contents for separate article on this topic.

The lounges in the Vista Dome cars are for cocktails . . . and viewing. Dining is in the refurbished Grand Dome, built in 1938, or the Northern Winds, built in 1949, or one of the other three fully restored cars. The five-course meal serves hors d'oeuvres, soup, salad, a choice of prime ribs or seafood or rock game hen, plus dessert, all as you glide through the country.

According to literature about the Minnesota Zephyr Ltd., "The Minnesota Zephyr, an elegant dining train, offers a chance to experience for the first time a journey back in time and, for some, the chance to relive and reminisce the era of the late 1940s. The Minnesota Zephyr has five dining cars carefully restored. Each car is different in design and color, recreating prestigious railroad dining of decades gone by. Both the afternoon and dinner excursions are identical. Each tour features a superb five-course, white linen dinner exquisitely prepared.

"For whatever your reasons . . . a very special occasion, a romantic rendezvous, or just a lasting memory."

Hours: Noon and 7:30, boarding an hour before. Reservations required **Phone**: 800-992-6100 **Admission**: $49.50 per person **Parking**: Ample in area **Address**: Minnesota Zephyr Ltd., 601 N. Main, P.O. Box 573, Stillwater, MN 55082

Fort Snelling State Park

The Fort Snelling State Park is located in the heart of the Twin Cities Metropolitan Area where the Minnesota and the Mississippi rivers converge. The state park adjoins the historic site of Fort Snelling* preserving important historical lands. The park harbors an abundance of wildlife which make their home among the forested river bottoms.

The park contains Pike Island, where Zebulon Pike set up his camp in September of 1805. Pike was in search of lands for possible military locations. He was able to obtain the land, and in 1821 Fort St. Anthony (later renamed Ft. Snelling) was built. On the island now is an Interpretive Center where naturalist programs are offered year-round. The programs vary from snowshoeing to maple sugaring to demonstrations on wildlife. In the Interpretive Center are wildlife exhibits which make the hike to Pike Island worthwhile. The state park system offers for children a Junior Naturalist program.

At the entrance of the park is the park headquarters where maps and information are available. The park offers 150 picnic sites with a shelter. There is a swimming beach and boat access to both lakes and rivers. During the summer there are eighteen miles of hiking trails, and these trails during the winter become cross-country ski trails. These trails wander along the river bottoms offering a very different view of the city and its origins. Here one can see the bottom of the Mendota Bridge and the base of Fort Snelling where settlers and Indians landed and traded. There are five miles of biking trails which can connect to Minnehaha Falls Park. The park also has a golf course and polo grounds.

Hours: The park is open year-round. During the summer it is closed from 10:00 p.m. to 8:00 a.m. At other times of the year the park closes at sunset. **Admission**: Daily or annual permits are required **Parking** Permitted in designated areas **Phone**: Park headquarters: (612) 727-1961, Pike Island Interpretive center: (612) 726-9247 **Address**: There is an entry on State Highway 5 just north of the airport a few

---

*   See Index or Contents for separate article on this topic.

hundred yards east of Hiawatha Avenue. There is another entry on Highway 5 just south of the main entrance to the airport.

Trolleys

There is an example of the wonderful streetcars, carefully restored, carefully maintained, and operating over a fifteen-minute, two-mile route from the west shore of Lake Harriet through Berry Park to the east shore of Lake Calhoun, a small bit of the old Como-Harriet line that ran from Como Park north of St. Paul to Fifty-fourth and France on the southwest corner of Minneapolis.

Streetcar tracks once were in every major street in the Twin Cities; you could go just about anywhere. The cars were big and yellow with a single headlight in the front and a trolley slanting up from the roof to roll along the overhead wire for electricity. Originally the back platform had no windows and thus was the place of banishment for smokers. There was a motorman who sat in front and did nothing but drive and change the switches. There was a conductor who stood in back and collected fares, gave out transfers, and tried to manage unruly boys. The seats and benches were of hard, varnished, woven straw that was impervious to stains and comfort.

These rails were in the middle of the street. Like a school bus, you were not allowed to pass them while their gates were open. Like school buses, they often had a long line of cars trailing behind them. If the snow was piled up on the side of the street, cars couldn't pass them at all. If a streetcar stalled for any reason, there would also be a long line of streetcars because they couldn't pass each other. It was a network that made the growth of the cities possible. Without them the transportation for the poor and middle class was by foot. Horses were expensive to buy and expensive to maintain. There were no stables for the factories the way there are parking lots now.

When the streetcars were replaced with buses, they were not mourned. Buses could also go anywhere but they could pull up to the curb for passengers and let cars pass. They could pass each other and change routes whenever necessary.

Now it is proposed to replace buses with streetcars—now called "light rail transit"—on main routes, recovering all the negatives.

Another and more glamorous streetcar of yore may also be coming back: the Streetcar Boats of Lake Minnetonka. They were designed to make business for the streetcar lines that stretched out to the lake. Once there were six of them connecting with the streetcars at Excelsior, Deephaven, and Wildhurst, then sailing to some twenty-seven ports on the lake. They were packed on Sundays and holidays. Men wore straw hats and long white pants and buttoned their suit coats. Women wore white, ankle-length dresses buttoned to the neck and wide-brimmed hats with ribbons. The little boys were supposed to sit quietly, the little girls did. It was a great adventure.

The last streetcar boat was scuttled in 1926, a victim to cars and boats. But in 1980 a group of volunteers raised it and is carefully restoring it to ply the waters once more. It can be seen at 140 George Street in Excelsior. No admission is charged but donations are never refused.

The volunteers have also restored the railway station at Minnehaha Park, which was once a stop on the main line coming in from Chicago. It was such a charming little depot that it was given the tile of "Princess."

The tireless volunteers are also restoring the Jackson Street Roundhouse at Jackson and Pennsylvania in St. Paul for use as their maintenance shops and as a museum for their memorabilia.

The Planes of Fame

This unique museum features military aircraft from WWII as well as a few biplanes from WWI. Unlike at other aircraft museums, such as the Smithsonian's Space and Aviation museum, here you will be seeing aircraft that are fueled and flight ready. That is because these planes are all flown regularly for airshows across the country and used in movie and television productions.

The Planes of Fame bearing the insignia of active World War II squadrons are displayed in honor of the men who flew, fought, and died in them. Most of the planes have been collected by Bob Pond and are lovingly cared for by a staff of 200 volunteers. These men and women conduct the tours, fly and maintain the aircraft (many of them come out every Thursday to clean them), and run the gift shop. They do this for the love they have for flying and for what these aircraft represent in American history. Many of them recently had the honor of meeting with the widow of Richard Bong on a visit to the museum. Bong, flying a P38 Lightning, was America's top flying ace of World War II.

There are over two dozen aircraft to see, displayed by the branch of service they flew in: the Army Air Corp, the Navy, or the Marines. Among the planes to be seen are the F6F-5 Hellcat, P51-D Mustang, P38 Lightning, and the FG-1D Corsair. Visitors to the museum are allowed to sit in the cockpit of the Corsair. Planes from other countries, the British Spitfire and the Russian Yak-11 trainer, are represented too. One special aircraft, a B-17 bomber which was attached to the 8th Air Force Volunteers, is available for an interior tour at an additional charge. Also to be seen are scale models of planes and ships, videos, munitions, medals, murals, and paintings.

Visitors may either go through the museum at their leisure or take one of the regularly scheduled tours. Tours may be led by Tom Lynburn, who is considered the museum's resident historian. Groups, especially schools, may schedule special tours. Children in sixth through eighth grades are particularly thrilled by visits to the museum. Two WWII Stearman trainers, which are open cockpit biplanes, are available for rides. The museum is in the process of setting up a course on aviation from a ground perspective.

The museum is open year-round with the exception of the B-17, which is flown south every winter (must be a snowbird).

Hours: 11:00-5:00 daily **Admission**: Adults $5, children 7-17 $2, children under 7 free. Call for tour times. **Phone**: 941-2633 **Address**: On the north side of Flying Cloud Airport on U.S. Highway 169 in Eden Prairie 55344

Bandana's Model Railroads

Formally called The Twin City Model Railroad Club, trains at Bandana Square model a panorama of railroading in the United States during its heyday in the 1930s, '40s and '50s. The Club originally started in 1935 in a store on Grand Avenue in St. Paul. In 1939 it moved to a room in the St. Paul Union Depot where it stayed until 1978. From then through 1984 it met at various members' homes and built a portable railroad for displays at shopping malls and Amtrak stations. Finally, in February 1984, the Club came to its current home in Bandana Square. By Thanksgiving of 1984 members had enough track down to start showing to the public. In February of 1985 they were able to open seven days per week. The Ramsey County Historical Society provides volunteers to run the railroads when the Club members aren't available. The Club's membership is now fifty-plus. New members are always welcome.

Trains are from the 1940 era, early diesel and late steam engine. Trains are a 1:48 "O" scale model railroad layout. That is 1/4" = 1 scale foot. Each main line is 220 real feet long or 2 scale miles! Up to five trains can operate at one time on the four main lines and the branchline. The north side of the railroad is an approximation of the "Palisades of the Mississippi River," complete with scenes of high bluffs and St. Anthony Falls milling district river frontage. It includes an incredible reproduction of the district, including the famous Stone Arch Bridge and three scale model, steel girder bridges that connected Minneapolis with St. Paul across the Mississippi River. The tracks enter a mural of Minneapolis dating back to when the Foshay Tower was the tallest building in the skyline. The mural was painted by Karen Remus, Art Services. Beyond that you're taken into the yards designed after the freight yard in St. Paul. Models of many famous trains can be seen during their special shows, including the Twin Cities Hiawatha, the North Coast Limited, the Zephyrs*, The Black Hawk, The Empire Builder, and the original '400,' to name a few.

More tunnels are on this railroad than all the railroad systems in the state of Minnesota. The reason for this is to move from one scene to another. Children of all ages love to see trains come out of the tunnels.

---

*   See Index or Contents for separate article on this topic.

Besides the large-scale model trains, the Club has on display possibly the best railroad pictures of any gallery in the Twin City area. It consists of contemporary paintings, old calendar paintings, and old advertisements from railroads.

Hours: Regular train operations: Monday-Friday 10:00-8:00, Saturday 10:00-6:00, Sunday noon-5:00 Saturday and Sunday are full operations days with trains running on all four mainlines under normal circumstances. **Phone**: (612) 647-9628. **Parking**: On-site **Admissions**: Donations encouraged. The entire Club income is dependent upon small membership dues and donations from public visitors. **Address**: Bandana Square just east of Snelling about a mile north of University Avenue in St. Paul 55104

The Minnesota Zoo

The Minnesota Zoo opened in 1978 on 500 acres in Burnsville in the southern metro area. Since opening, it has entertained, educated, and delighted millions of visitors. It is home to 2,700 mammals, birds, fish, reptiles, and amphibians. Besides the trails to explore and the animals to touch, there are special events, programs, and demonstrations to see. No matter what time of year, the zoo has much to offer.

The zoo has developed beyond just a place to view animals. It is a member of the International Capture Breeding Specialist Group and International Species Information System and participates in species survival plans. One program has been to work with the Department of Natural Resources (DNR) and Hennepin County Parks to release the endangered trumpeter swans into the wild. The zoo has begun to create a special summer exhibit beyond the daily exhibits. First there was the Dinosaur Park then the Bugs Park. What will be next?

Upon entering the zoo, a visitor can choose from among six diverse trails to explore. The Tropics Trail abounds with lush vegetation and animals found in the warmer climates. The trail wanders below the animals to the popular coral reef. Here visitors can watch the fish and marine animals at their level below the water surface. Special fun is to watch the feeding. Children press against the glass to decide which color or shaped fish they like best. As the trail emerges back to the tropics, nighttime animals are on view.

The Ocean Trail is another favorite which goes below to view sea creatures and the dolphins. Plan to spend some time watching the playful antics of the dolphins. During the summer seasons the dolphins and their show can be viewed from the stands around their tank.

The Minnesota Trail features the wildlife natural to this region. The animals are exhibited in natural surroundings such as the water pond for the beaver.

The Northern Trail wanders around the grounds of the zoo. Visitors can see animals from the northern hemisphere in natural habitat. Along the trail is the Zoofari Park which hosts a playground and resting areas. Look for the amphitheater which hosts the World of Birds show or listen to the summer evening concerts.

The Discovery Trail is a must for families. The focus is the children's zoo. Here animals may be touched and are exhibited so children can get up close.

Skytrail is a monorail which takes the visitor over the northern trail. Riders can sit back and listen to a natural history narrative.

The Zoolab is a must for children. Here volunteers show off animals and supervise young hands and minds, touching and learning about the animals on display.

The zoo abounds with special programs such as family zoo adventures, overnights, zoo camp, adult programs, adult education, teacher workshops, preschool programs, and zoo discovery programs.

Hours: 10:00-6:00 April-September, 10:00-4:00 October-March **Phone**: 432-9000
Parking: Ample on site **Admission**: Adults $5, senior citizens $3, children 3-12 $2
Address: 13000 Zoo Blvd., Apple Valley 55337

Como Park and Zoo

St. Paul is home to lions, tigers, leopards, cougars, gorillas, orangutans, giraffes, zebras, antelopes, polar bears, seals, penguins, sea lions, bison, goats, and wolves. These animals and others make up the over 350 residents of Como Zoo.

In 1873 the city of St. Paul acquired 300 acres to be set aside for park land. This land became Como Park and Como Zoo. By 1893 an electric railway reached the boundaries of the Park making it easily accessible. By 1897 the Park had miles of paths and wonderful gardens. This was the year that three deer were given to the city. Pasture land at the Park was fenced in and Como Zoo was started.

The first major construction at the zoo began in the 1930s as WPA projects. This included the main building, a bear grotto, monkey island, and a barn. However, by 1955 the city of St. Paul recommended closing the zoo. A volunteer committee succeeded in saving the zoo. After that the seal show started, the animal collection was expanded, a children's zoo was created, and a private house and wolf woods were added. Then once again by 1966 the Como Zoo was in trouble. There was not enough space to enlarge into a major facility, but another emergency committee was formed to save the zoo. A master plan was developed and the funds were raised.

In the 1970s redevelopment and renovation were started. The lions and tigers were the first to receive a new home, then Sparky the seal's Seal Island was renovated. Because of the extreme weather of Minnesota, Como Zoo has created indoor viewing areas for the non-northern climate animals.

Como Zoo is an adventure for youngsters. It is a small facility, making it easier to see the animals and experience the entire zoo. While at the Como Zoo, visit the Conservatory and the gardens. The beautiful flowers and plants make for a nice retreat in January.

Hours: October-March 8:00-5:00 for the grounds and 10:00-4:00 for the buildings, April-September 8:00-8:00 for the grounds and 10:00-6:00 for the buildings.
Phone: 487-0388 **Parking**: On-site **Admission**: Free **Address**: Como at Lexington, east of the Fairgrounds, North St. Paul 55117

Murphy's Landing

Murphy's Landing is a living history museum of Minnesota life from 1840 to 1890. The museum was created on the Minnesota River along eighty-seven acres of woods and trails in the late 1960s to preserve land along the Minnesota River and the historic buildings of the area and to allow guests to step back in time and share the lifestyles of the immigrant settlers. The land was part of a site owned by a Colonel Murphy, who operated an inn and a boat crossing. Murphy had hoped that his village would develop, but the railroad went further downstream.

The museum starts out at the Visitors' Center. There is a walking trail to guide the visitor through the decades starting at the trading post, past the school, the herb garden, the depot, the church, and the blacksmith, to name only a few of the stops along the way. Most stops are staffed by volunteers portraying Minnesota River Valley residents, knowledgeable and more than willing to converse as they go about their activities. There are several additional buildings which are under renovation.

Murphy's Landing hosts a variety of special events throughout the year. Some of the events are Civil War Days, a Celtic festival, a country fair, a fiddle contest, a crafts weekend, a demonstration of a typical woman's work day, and a candlelight tour. An outstanding feature for the whole family is Folkways of Christmas, in which the different buildings are decorated according to various Christmas traditions of the nationalities represented by the settlers to Minnesota.

Visitors may walk the grounds and the nature trails or ride on the horse-drawn trolley. The old depot has a gift shop, and the country store has many period items for sale. For the visitor who has developed an appetite, Murphy's Fine Foods Restaurant provides fun family dining.

Also available is a narrated boat tour along the Minnesota River provided by Creative River Tours. These tours can be taken separately or as part of a package.

Hours: May: Sundays 10:00-5:00; Summer: Tuesday-Sunday 10:00-5:00; September and October: weekends 10:00-5:00 **Phone**: 445-6900 **Parking**: Available on the grounds **Admission**: Adults $7, seniors and children 6-17 $6, children under 6 free **Address**: Highway 101 east of Shakopee

The Gibbs Farm

In the spring of 1849 Herman and Jane Gibbs purchased a 160-acre tract of land for $1.25 per acre in what is now the city of Falcon Heights. They built a sod house which was their home for five years. In 1854 they built a log home which was added on to in 1867 and again in the 1870s. Their history can be viewed at the Gibbs Farm Museum, which has been operated by the Ramsey County Historical Society since 1954. The farm is open to the public for tours. It includes the farmhouse, a schoolhouse from 1870s, a barn built around 1900, and another one built in 1958. The seven-acre site includes beautiful gardens and fields for the sheep, chickens, pigs, cats, and the horse.

The farmstead is decorated and maintained in the era of 1910. There is a large collection of farming, veterinary, woodworking, and fiber arts equipment along with many household items. In the house is a "touch-and-feel" room where children can play with and try items from another era.

The staff and volunteers of the farm are present to give tours of the house, demonstrate activities such as blacksmithing, and answer questions. They also host Sunday programs which accentuate life at the turn of the century. These events are designed so that the entire family can participate and enjoy.

The museum is an easily accessible place to go back in time. It is visited by many daycare facilities and schools.

Gibbs Farm also represents the first project of the Ramsey County Historical Society. The society wanted to save the farm and worked out an agreement with the University of Minnesota, which had purchased the farm from the Gibbs family in 1943. Many of the possessions of the Gibbs family were sold or given away. The Historical Society was able to recover some of them.

Hours: Tuesday-Friday 10:00-4:00; Saturdays, Sundays, and holiday Mondays noon-4:00 May-October **Phone**: 646-8629 **Admission**: Adults $2.50, seniors $2, children $1 **Parking**: Ample on the site **Address**: 2097 West Larpenteur Ave, St. Paul

The Original Baseball Hall of Fame Museum

Baseball aficionados must visit this free museum across the street from the Metrodome's north side. It was originally founded in 1986 with the private collection of Ray Crump. Crump has been collecting baseball memorabilia for over fifty years. He started as a bat boy for the Washington Senators and moved with the team to Minneapolis in 1961 as equipment manager until 1984.

The collection includes autographs as well as signed baseballs, baseball cards, uniforms, and bats, among many other items. There is also a display on how bats are made. The walls are adorned with pictures of all the celebrities Crump and his family have encountered. The museum is an exceptional place to buy baseball souvenirs.

Hours: Monday-Friday, 9:00-5:00, Saturday 11:00-3:00. Open during Dome events. **Admission**: Free **Phone**: 375-9707 **Address**: Fifth Street and Tenth Avenue, Minneapolis 55487

The Children's Museum

The Children's Museum was founded in 1979 in a renovated warehouse in Minneapolis, then moved to Bandana Square in St. Paul. The museum relocated once again to the corner of Seventh and Wabash streets in the heart of downtown St. Paul, near the World Trade Center and the Science Museum. This allowed an increase in total square footage from 18,000 square feet to 65,000 square feet. The grand opening of the new museum took place in the fall of 1995.

The mission of the museum is to promote hands-on, interactive learning for children. This plan provides parents, teachers, and care providers with experience in participatory education while stimulating the curiosity of children about themselves and the world.

The new Minnesota Children's Museum has been carefully planned to place the world into the hands of the children who visit. The museum currently offers a vast variety of exhibits that promote cooperation with others and for individual learning; hands-on fun and quiet times for reflection; and finally (and most of all), excitement.

Some of the elements of the new museum will include: "World of Wonder," "Earth World," "One World," "World Works," "Habitot," and much more.

In "World of Wonder," fantasy and fact are combined for children and adults for exploration of their own senses.

"Earth World" will promote awareness of the environment using vivid and engaging exhibits. You will be transformed into an ant, enabling you to climb through a huge ant hill maze. Additionally, you will get a fish eye's view when going "underwater" in the pond to view food, home, and neighbors. Discover how the plants and animals change throughout Minnesota seasons in the "Forest."

The Children's Museum is located in expanded quarters at Seventh and Wabasha in St. Paul, 55101. It is open Tuesday-Sunday 9:00-5:00. Call 644-5305 for more information.

The Ellingson Car Museum

This museum is more than just a display of cars lined up as if in a dealer's lot. A lot of loving care has been taken to depict the automobile's role in American culture since the inception of mass-produced cars. As you move through the museum you are transported, era by era, from the teens to the '80s through scenes of popular American automotive culture.

Although some of the cars are unique and costly or are important by virtue of having been owned by a celebrity, including a 1954 Kaiser Darin and a 35 Mercedes 500SSK (a steal at $900,000), many of the cars displayed were production models for their particular era. Many of the cars are in original condition, though obviously well taken care of, while others are restored. Some of the cars are rotated on a six-month basis so that there is always something "new" to see on repeat visits.

Before you even enter the museum, there is a display of fine cars and motorcycles in the foyer, some rated at "perfect" restored condition. As you enter the museum you are immediately transported to the '20s and '30s. A video shows an early Ford factory amidst a collection of Tin Lizzies. Packards, Fords, Dodges, and Chevrolets of the '30s are displayed in a setting of vintage memorabilia, including porcelain signs, gas pumps, and photographs.

Since car production was halted during WWII, a small display of military vehicles produced by automobile companies represents the early '40s. One of the more unique exhibits of this period is Chrysler's thirty-cylinder mystery engine which powered the Sherman tank. This engine is actually five six-cylinder engines linked together in synchronization. It mystifies the onlookers!

Next stop is the '50s featuring a mock-up of a drive-in movie theater, where cars, replete with popcorn and fuzzy dice, are lined up in front of the big screen showing vintage movie trailers. What period car museum would be complete without a used car lot! Completing the '50s exhibit is Fast Eddie's used auto sales alongside period TV and radio.

The muscle cars of the '60s and '70s are lined up in a drag strip rendition featuring vintage starting lights. Stock cars, dragsters, and rods are mixed together for this race. GTO's, Impalas, and Roadrunners are featured as well as a few unique limited production models.

Rounding out the displays are various motorcycles, pickups, and a 1951 Snow Flyer (the great granddaddy of the snowmobile) and a small area where some cars are for sale.

At the end of your tour you can stop at the '50s-era vending lounge and visit the gift shop. Be sure and stop to see the collection of grille ornaments.

The Ellingson car museum is available for parties and has a meeting room for car clubs.

Hours: Monday-Saturday 10:00-6:00, Sunday 12:00-5:00 **Phone**: 428-7337 **Parking**: On-site **Admission**: Free **Address**: The Ellingson museum is located 20 minutes northwest of downtown Minneapolis at the Rogers exit off I-94.

The Firefighters Memorial Museum

Tucked away in an old warehouse in northeast Minneapolis is the Firefighters Museum, a wonderful experience for one and all but especially for the young.

The museum houses everything from antique firefighting equipment to modern-day equipment. They have on display old trucks, pumps, bells, hoses, and all sorts of other firefighting equipment. The displays show the progress firefighting has made over the past century. Several antique trucks are available for climbing and exploring. A replica of a fire station office shows how fires were reported. There is also an area which has firefighting clothes and boots for children to try on and to play pretend.

Along with the wonderful equipment there is a video demonstration showing how fast a fire can destroy a room. The volunteers at the museum wish not only to entertain but also to educate about fire. As a final part of the admission the ride on the back of a fire truck can be the highlight for any kid.

The museum has a small but good selection of firefighting memorabilia to view or for purchase. A small library area can also accommodate birthday parties.

Hours: Saturday 9:00-3:00 **Phone**: 623-3817 **Parking**: Nearby **Admission**: $2 for children, $4 for adults **Address**: 1100 NE Van Buren, Minneapolis 55413

Lock and Dam #1

On the Mississippi River, just below St. Anthony Falls and above Fort Snelling, is Lock and Dam #1, often called the "Ford Dam." In 1899 the Congress authorized the building of the locks and dam to improve navigation on the river between Minneapolis and St. Paul. Construction was completed in 1917.

The walk to the dam on the west side of the river is peaceful while descending to the river. The river is calm, beautiful, and a boaters' paradise.

From the Visitor Promenade at Locks and Dam #1 visitors get a bird's-eye view of the locking procedure and a dramatic look at the 674-foot-long dam. The promenade takes you up approximately three stories above the locks to provide a multitude of wonderful views not only of the locks but of the entire river. The Visitor Promenade is open to the public every day April through October from 8:00 a.m. until 10:00 p.m.

Across the river in 1923 the Ford Motor Company was granted a license to construct a power plant. Enough power is generated to supply the Ford Motor Company, the locks, and to supplement local needs.

Hours: April-October 8:00 a.m.-10:00 p.m. **Parking**: Nearby **Admission**: Free **Address**: West River Road at Ford Bridge

The Minnesota Landscape Arboretum

In the bustle and hustle of today's world the Minnesota Landscape Arboretum offers a fantastic refuge, a place to regroup and relax. It is a wonderful place to take a hike, have a picnic, enjoy a waterfall, or smell some flowers.

The Arboretum was established in 1958 as a part of the University of Minnesota's Department of Horticultural Science. It is spread over 900 beautifully landscaped acres with more than 5,000 species and cultivars of plants.

A visit to the Arboretum needs to start with the Snyder Building. This beautiful building houses the Andersen Horticultural Library with 9,500 volumes, a gift shop, a conservatory, and a tearoom offering delicious soups and treats. Beginning at the Snyder Building, walking trails wind through the various gardens. For the gardener it is a treat to wander through these gardens. There are gardens specializing in annuals, perennials, herbs, azaleas, hostas, and a Japanese garden, just to name a few. Besides a walk through the gardens, one can hike trails through birch and ash trees, along a bog, or through other research areas of the Arboretum.

The facilities of the Arboretum are open all year. An education department offers programs and classes for all levels. Classes are offered in gardening and landscaping, and children's field trips are welcomed. The staff conducts ongoing research on cold-hardy plants with recent developments in the Northern Lights azalea series, honeysuckle, apples, and maples, to name a few. More than seventy cold-hardy fruit varieties have been introduced since the Horticultural Research Center was founded in 1908.

The seasons of Minnesota are celebrated with many ongoing programs and special events. Springtime celebrates the awakening of the plants. Hikes along the trails abound in new colors and fresh scents. The annual plant sale adds to the gardeners' excitement. Summer provides the richness of all the plants from the luxuriant greens to the full color blooms. Hikes through the cool hosta gardens and trails compliment the warmth of the annual gardens. Summer brings the Mid-China Festival and a Children's Harvest Fest. Autumn, with the last burst of color, is spectacular at the Arboretum. It is a wonderful time to explore the trails, especially the woodland trails. The Fall Festival has many activities for all and great fun for families.

Hours: Grounds: 8:00 a.m. to sunset; building & library: Monday-Friday 8:00-4:30; weekends and holidays: 11:00-4:30 **Admission**: Adults $4, children 6-15 $1, children under 5 free. **Phone**: 443-2460 **Address**: 3675 Arboretum Drive, Chanhassen 55317

Historic Fort Snelling

As you enter Fort Snelling itself, be ready to join the men and women of the 5th Regiment of Infantry. The time is the 1840s and Fort Snelling is the most northwestern post of the young United States. Greeting you are costumed guides who present a vivid picture of life on the frontier. They'll be glad to talk to you but, since they are portraying 1843, they know nothing of anything that happened after that.

Take the time to explore the fort and the many exhibits. Guided tours are available or you can pick up a map for a self-guided tour. Within the fort, wander through the buildings to learn more about pioneer life. There is the first school in Minnesota which also served as the first church. The guardhouse was the police and the fire station of the fort, equipped with two dark cells. The magazine was designed to be a secure, dry, and cool place for ammunition. The fort has three batteries and a round tower. These were designed as a defensive strong point. Climbing up into them provides wonderful views of the surrounding area. There is a sutler's store to supply the soldiers and settlers with goods brought up the river in the once-a-month trip from St.

Louis. There are two sets of barracks for the enlisted men. One of the barracks houses interesting exhibits documenting the life of nineteenth-century soldiers. The Commandant's House is situated at one corner of the fort with an impressive view of the river. The officers had twelve sets of quarters for themselves and their families. There was also a space for plays and parties. At one end of the building, an archeology exhibit showing the original 1820s foundation can be seen. Along the last wall of the fort is the building which housed the first hospital in the state. Finally there are the bakery, the blacksmith, the wheelwright, the armorer, and the harness shops. These areas are maintained with all the tools and equipment of the period, with people demonstrating them.

The fort had fallen into decay, new buildings had been erected over the years, and original buildings were destroyed. But after the threat of a freeway in 1956, Fort Snelling in 1960 was designated the state's first National Historic Landmark. Using both public and private money, the fort has been reconstructed as it existed in the 1820s.

Fort Snelling History Center is at the entrance to the fort. They have a wonderful museum store and offer a short movie on the park. The center is host to public programs on World War II, First Minnesota Volunteer Infantry, Living History Society of Minnesota, La Compagnie, Minnesota Air National Guard Museum, and Military and Arms Museum of Minnesota.

Hours: Historic Fort Snelling: May-October Monday-Friday 10:00-5:00, Sunday noon-5:00. Closed November-April. Fort Snelling History Center: May-October daily 9:30-5:00, November-April weekdays 9:00-4:30 **Admission**: Historic Fort Snelling: Adults $3, children 6-15 $1, children 5 and under free. Fort Snelling History Center is free. **Phone**: 726-1171 **Address**: State Highway 5 north of the airport, a few hundred yards east of Hiawatha Avenue

The Raptor Center

Injured birds of prey (raptors, such as eagles, hawks, falcons) have a world class treatment and care facility in St. Paul. The Raptor Center was started in 1972 in a facility at the University of Minnesota and has since moved to its larger present site. The primary goals of the Center are rehabilitation and research; education is also of primary importance.

The Raptor Center treats some 600 birds each year. These birds arrive from all over the Upper Midwest and the country. The staff tries to treat and rehabilitate these birds. If the patient can fully recover, it is released back to the wild, but some are too badly injured and are given a home and a "job" in the education program.

Tours are given Monday through Saturday by reservation. The tours last about 45 minutes and include a slide show, information about raptors, and presentations of live birds. Some tours may include the education courtyard, but weather and the group may prohibit it. Tours are geared to the group, and school tours are certainly welcome.

At the Center there are several exhibits of live birds. These permanent residents of the Center tour schools and other community organizations to get out the message on the environment and the importance of raptors. Each spring and fall the Raptor Center sponsors public bird releases.

Hours: Monday-Friday 9:00-4:00, Saturday 11:00-4:00 **Tours**: $3 for adults, $2 for seniors, and $1.50 for children **Phone**: 624-4745 **Parking**: Nearby **Admission**: Free **Address**: 1920 Fitch Avenue on the St. Paul Campus of the University of Minnesota 55109

The Alexis Bailly Vineyard

Everyone knows that it's too cold in Minnesota to grow grapes for wine! Except for a few devoted souls. In 1973 Alexis Bailly planted his first vines in the lush Hiawatha Valley of the Upper Mississippi. In 1977 he produced the first wine ever made entirely from Minnesota-grown grapes. He's progressed from there.

Drawing courtesy of the Alexis Baily Vineyard

According to a brochure about the vineyard:

Because of the uniqueness of climate and soil in each part of the world, planting grapes where they have never grown before is inherently difficult. In most other areas of the United States, grape growers started by looking for vines that could most easily be grown without regard to their ultimate wine quality. This invariably made the grower's job easy but the wine maker's job impossible. Because of this, many parts of the United States and Canada developed the reputation of producing mediocre or at best, average wines.

At Alexis Bailly it was started the opposite way. That is, a search was made for the best quality wine grapes. Then an attempt to get them to grow was made. This has resulted in many problems for the grower, especially in getting vines to survive the extreme winters. Vines must be trained with long diagonal trunks so that before winter they can be laid on the ground and covered with dirt or mulch. Only by such practices can vines survive Minnesota winters.

On the other hand, such practices have allowed Minnesota to produce premium quality wines. When you have good grapes you make good wine. In six of the last seven years the wines of Alexis Bailly have won international awards of merit and have received critical approval both in this country and in Europe. This is because only the best of wine grapes possible are grown.

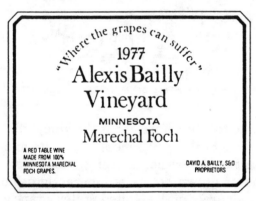

Drawing courtesy of the Alexis Baily Vineyard

The emphasis has always been on trying to produce the best wine possible with Minnesota grown grapes. Thus the awards that have been won and the critical acclaim received is even more significant because it is in recognition of the quality of a completely new viticultural area.

Each year wineries from all over the United States and Canada come together for an international competition called "Wineries Unlimited." It has allowed each winery to determine how its wines stack up against all of the other wines being produced. In a normal year, there are over 600 wines submitted to the competition. Alexis Bailly has won twelve awards, including on three occasions the award of "best of its class."

Hours: Noon-5:00 Friday-Sunday, June-October **Phone**: 437-1413 **Parking**: On-site **Admission**: Free **Address**: 18200 Kirby Avenue, Hastings 55033. Watch for signs on U.S. Hwy. 61.

Northern Vineyards

In 1979 Wisconsin horticulturist Elmer Swenson, who had been working with vines for several decades, introduced seven varieties to the Stillwater area and proved that they could survive and succeed and add more to the joy of living in the Twin Cities Metropolitan Area.

Mr. Swenson's hybrids ripen fruit early, well within the short Minnesota growing season, and are much more tolerant of the winters than the French-American hybrids which have to be cut from their trellises, laid on the ground, and covered with soil or straw and then uncovered and tied back up as soon as the snow melts.

The Twin Cities are at the same latitude as the Bordeaux region of France and much farther south than the Rhine areas of Germany. There is the same rolling wooded hillsides next to streams and lakes and the same sunshine. The only impediment has been the continental climate with early and harsh winters. But these are overcome by tipping the vines and by developing hybrids.

Northern Vineyards actually has its vines all over the state, wherever site and soil, sun and rain are found in the right combinations. The vineyards are small but carefully tended by members of the Minnesota Winegrowers Cooperative. It produces nine wines, some dry and sweet white wines, some blushes, and some full-bodied reds.

Hours: January-April Tuesday-Saturday 10:00-5:00, Sunday 12:00-5:00; May-December Monday-Saturday 10:00-5:00, Sunday 12:00-5:00 **Phone**: 430-1032 **Parking**: On-site **Admission**: Free **Address**: Staples Sawmill, 402 North Main Street, Stillwater 55082 (in Stillwater just north of the bridge)

Hennepin County Parks

Hennepin County operates a system of fourteen parks, encompassing 25,000 acres, which are managed to provide recreational activities for everyone while protecting the sensitive environment, an often imposing conflict. The numerous activities include hiking, skiing, biking, camping, swimming, boating, golfing, and picnicking.

There is a strong focus on family activities as well as programs for individuals. There are three interpretive nature centers offering programs for individuals and families. Other family highlights of the parks are the six creative play areas which offer a child hours of fun and learning, with their slides, ladders, multilevel platforms, bridges, and tunnels that have to be seen and tried to be appreciated. There is an annual outdoor family celebration known as "Prairie Fest," a free event which celebrates and promotes public awareness of the unique grasslands and prairies of Minnesota.

Memberships are available which include a quarterly magazine highlighting all the activities and events in the parks. The events can be as wide-ranged as monarch butterfly tagging, collecting wildflower seeds, fungi foraging, or full moon hikes.

The Twin Cities area has always been blessed with an extensive park system, though the Hennepin County Parks have only been in existence for thirty-eight years. The parks system began in 1956 with a gift of 210 acres by Morris T. Baker on Lake Independence in western Hennepin. The continued acquisition of lands came through funds from bond issues, first of $250,000 and then an additional $8 million. The parks also received gifts of land along the Minnesota River, Coon Rapids Dam, and Lake Minnetonka.

Here is a listing of the Hennepin County parks. Check out the map for the new bike trails throughout the county:

Baker Park Reserve
west central Hennepin County 476-4666

This is the first in the system, dating back to 1956. Within its current 2,700 acres, there are 10k of paved bike trails and 11.5k of cross-country ski trails. Swimming, picnicking, golfing, boating, and fishing can all be enjoyed by the day or while camping out in the public campground. Baker Park also boasts of the first creative play area which was constructed in the summer of 1977.

Bryant Lake Regional Park
south central Hennepin County 941-4362

The 170-acre Bryant Lake Park has been newly redeveloped on Bryant Lake with its beautiful sand bottom, offering swimming, boating, and fishing. There is a public picnic area with a pavilion in case of rain.

Carver Park Reserve
northwestern Carver County 472-4911

Carver Park is home to the Lowry Nature Center which opened in January of 1969 and was the first of the three nature centers. The park has 3,300 acres supporting a wide variety of wildlife and preserving an abundance of natural resources. The nature center is able to capitalize on all these resources and offer programs ranging from maple syrup making to stargazing to Halloween Haunts. The park includes four lakes for boating and fishing, picnic areas, and a public campground. There are many kilometers of hiking, biking, and cross-country ski trails with bike and ski rentals available.

Cleary Lake Regional Park
north central Scott County 447-2171

The 1,045-acre Cleary Lake Park is located in the southern metro area. This park opened in May of 1977. It is highlighted by the sandy swimming beach and the boating and fishing which makes it a great place for picnics. The park has a par-3 nine-hole golf course and a driving range. The 13.3k of groomed cross-country ski trails make for great sport in the winter.

Coon Rapids Dam Regional Park
west central Anoka County 424-8172

This 610-acre park opened in August of 1979 and is situated alongside the Mississippi River. The park offers an up-close view of the river with access for boating and fishing. Access to the North Hennepin Regional Trail Corridor can be gained through the park. The Trail Corridor provides over 11k of hiking, biking, and cross-country skiing.

Crow-Hassan Park Reserve
northwestern Hennepin County 476-4666

Crow-Hassan Park has 2,600 acres which are representative of the prairies the early settlers crossed. The Crow River makes a boundary of the park as well as a boundary of Hennepin and Wright counties. There are group campsites available along the river and 19k of hiking and horseback trails and 17k of groomed cross-country ski trails. These trails wander through the prairie and the beautiful woodlands.

Elm Creek Park Reserve
northern Hennepin County 424-5511

This park with 4,900 acres is the largest in the Hennepin County Park system. Elm Creek is home to the Eastman Nature Center (420-4300) which has exhibits and programming making use of the abundance of wildlife. The park has enough activities to keep the most active person or family busy throughout the day. There are many kilometers of hiking, biking, and cross-country ski trails. Families can enjoy the creative play area, go swimming, and feast on a picnic lunch.

Fish Lake Regional Park
north central Hennepin County 420-3423

This small 160-acre wooded park offers the water sports of fishing, boating, and swimming. There are hiking and biking trails with in-line skates available for rental.

French Regional Park
central Hennepin County 559-8891

French Regional Park is named for Cliff French, the self-effacing Hennepin Park Director who labored hard to build and develop the whole system from its beginnings. It is located on 310 acres on Medicine Lake with a variety of water-based activities. The park offers monthly outdoor education programs featuring topics of maple syruping and beaver lodges. Along with the hiking, biking, and skiing trails there is also a creative play area.

Hyland Lake Park Reserve
southern Hennepin County 941-4362

Hyland Lake Park was opened in the fall of 1964 and is spread out over 1,000 acres in Bloomington. The park is home to the Richardson Nature Center (941-7993) with beautiful trails through the woods and opportunities to see deer, pheasants, birds, and many other forms of wildlife. The nature center, which opened in September of 1970, offers year-round programs for all ages. The park has extensive recreational facilities including hiking, biking, and cross-country ski trails. There is swimming, boating, and fishing with boat, bike, and ski rentals available. The creative play area has the nickname of Chutes and Ladders and is surrounded by beautiful picnic grounds. The Hyland Hills ski area is located within the park.

Lake Rebecca Park Reserve
western Hennepin County 476-4666

This park surrounds Lake Rebecca and is bordered by the Crow River, making it a haven for wildlife, which can be viewed from the 21k of turf hiking trails or the 10k of paved bike and hiking trails. The lake offers excellent fishing and boating.

Murphy-Hanrehan Park Reserve
northern Scott County 447-2171

This 2,400-acre park is largely undeveloped with the exception of the trail system. The park does offer 19k of groomed cross-country trails designed for the intermediate to the advanced skier. There are also 15k of horseback trails.

Norenberg Memorial Park
west central Hennepin County 476-4666

This small gem of a park was the former Lake Minnetonka estate of Frederick Norenberg. It is a reminder of days gone by with excellent views of Lake Minnetonka. The beautiful and carefully maintained formal flower gardens and cute gazebo on the lake shore are pleasant for ambling and find frequent use for weddings. No other facilities are available.

Hours: General park hours are from 5:00 until sunset. Hours may vary according to specific programs at the nature centers, visitor centers, and the trailheads. **Phone**: 559-9000 **Admission**: Free **Parking**: Daily parking fees are $4 or 12-month parking permit for $20 **Address**: North of Lake Minnetonka's Crystal Bay on County Road 15

Minneapolis and Saint Paul Park Systems

The two cities have some ninety-three parks between them including eight golf courses, numerous parkways, and major centers. Mostly the parks are designed to fit a particular neighborhood rather than to have area appeal. The large parks with broad appeal, such as Como, Chain of Lakes, and Minnehaha, are treated separately in previous sections, as are Anoka's parks and the county and state parks. Information and maps about the neighborhood parks can be had from the St. Paul Park Department at 266-6400 or the Minneapolis Park Department at 661-4800.

Hiking and Biking Trails

All of the large parks described in this section have trails for both hiking and biking, usually with maps provided at the park's center. On the following page is a map of the Grand Rounds Trail in Minneapolis, a challenge to anyone and of considerable interest as it winds around seven lakes and the Mississippi River.

Snowmobile Trails

Most large parks maintain snowmobile trails with maps available at the park's center.

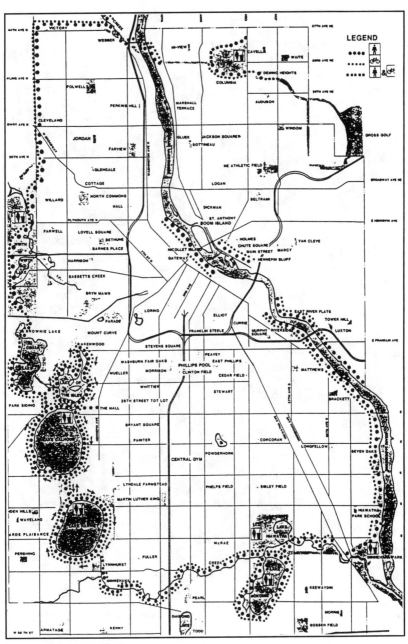

Hiking and Biking Trails

Snowmobile Trails

CHAPTER 8

Stages and Theaters

The Ordway

"Jewel." The word that almost universally comes to mind for the Ordway Theater in the center of St. Paul, with Rice Park as its setting and Landmark Center*, the Hill-St. Paul Library*, and the St. Paul hotel as its protectors. It's a jewel by day, its facets designed to reflect its illustrious neighbors, and by night when it quietly blends the darkness with the city lights. ". . . a theater where music infuses and inspires the environment—where harmonies are for both eye and ear, where sound and vision, color and light, flow together in an artful unity of theater and life," according to a theater brochure. Ben Thompson is its principal architect.

The brochure further states:

Inside, the building projects a romantic ambiance. The patron is drawn by the sweeping spiral stair, the "Grand Stair," that leads to the Grand Foyer. The stair continues on up to an Upper Promenade that surrounds the Main Hall balcony. From all

---

* See Index or Contents for separate article on this topic.

three levels, there are spectacular views outside of the historic buildings on Rice Park, the city skyline, and across the Mississippi.

In the grand tradition of the European opera house, the Ordway's Main Hall is designed in a horseshoe shape, with three shallow curving balconies ending in tiers of boxes close to the stage. This is an intimate yet imposing space. It has been described as a "baroque hall setting in a warm contemporary design" and as "the most contemporary classic theater in the United States."

The interior design . . . enhances the elegance of the basic design. Large wall sconces shed light around the curving walls and latticework panels, while Honduran mahogany doors, accented with brass, complement the rust, blue, and gold interior. A custom-woven carpet of patterned royal blue extends up the aisles and out into the lobbies.

It is home to the renowned St. Paul Chamber Orchestra, the Schubert Club, and the Minnesota Opera. It is regularly used by the Minnesota Orchestra, which is among the best. In the Main Hall as well as in the smaller rehearsal and audition halls, numerous musicals, plays, and shows are performed.

Hours: Set by performances **Phone**: 224-4222 **Parking**: Nearby ramps **Admission**: Set by performance **Address**: 345 Washington Street, St. Paul 55102

The Guthrie

The following appears in a Guthrie Theater pamplet:
There were many people in the American theater who questioned Guthrie's choice of the Twin Cities

as the site of a major classical repertory theater. Guthrie cites his reasons for the choice: the location of the Twin Cities in the heartland of America, the vitality of their general cultural activity, the presence of a large state university and the many small private colleges, and the spontaneous enthusiasm shown by the Upper Midwest community for the new theater project.

Over the years, the Guthrie has had several different directors and therefore several different styles. Under Guthrie's direction in its first year, it presented Shakespeare's *Hamlet*, Chekov's *The Three Sisters*, and Miller's *Death of a Salesman*. In 1969 it became the first regional theater to go on a national tour, playing successfully in Los Angeles and New York. Under Liviu Ciulei, it received a Tony Award in 1982, and in 1985 Guthrie productions reached national acclaim for *The Tempest*, *Peer Gynt* (staged in two parts), and *Midsummer Night's Dream*, named by *Time* magazine as one of the year's best.

In 1992 it received the ultimate acclaim of its audiences: $26,114,345 was pledged to its Campaign for Artistic Excellence, including an unprecedented 4,519 individual pledges of more than half the total. Its remodeling has been completed with a bigger lobby and more women's restrooms. It has 1,308 seats in a 180-degree arc around the stage, no seat being more than fifty-two feet from the actors.

Employing some 300 people at the height of the season, the Guthrie is internationally known for the high artistic and technical standards it maintains in its work and its operations. With a variety of shops and workrooms, the theater constructs on a major scale. Sets, costumes, wigs, millinery, jewelry, furniture, masks, armor, and weaponry, and a wide variety of props ranging from a birdcage to a collapsible piano are all built in the five-level backstage area. Only shoes are bought from the outside—to be remade by Guthrie crafts people in accordance with the costume designer's sketches.

The Guthrie has reached out to the community. It has a youth program which, among other activities, widely distributes free tickets to children so they can have the opportunity to experience live theater. It has established the Guthrie Laboratory in the Warehouse District* to provide a facility to explore and develop new work and performance techniques with the purpose of enhancing the actors' skills.

Hours: Usual theater times **Phone**: 377-2224 **Parking**: Nearby lot **Admission**: $9.00-$42.00, depending on the day of the week and time of the day **Address**: Vineland Place, Minneapolis 55403 (next to the Walker Art Center* on Hennepin and across from the Sculpture Garden*)

Orchestra Hall

It was designed for music! Not for theater, not for sports, not for political gatherings, just music. It does it very well. A whisper on stage can be heard in any of the 2,462 seats, even the ones at the back of the third tier. The sight lines are unimpeded, unless the lady in front of you is wearing a big hat. The seats are comfortable; some patrons have even been known to doze. And the music is spectacular! According to Orchestra Hall pamplet:

---

*   See Index or Contents for separate article on this topic.

When Orchestra Hall opened on October 21, 1974, a new chapter of art and entertainment in the Upper Midwest began. The acoustically acclaimed modern concert hall, located on the Nicollet Mall in downtown Minneapolis, quickly became a major performance center, one of the busiest in the country. As the home of the Minnesota Orchestra, it is the site of year-round symphony concerts, pops programs, a summer festival, and children's concerts, all featuring the Minnesota Orchestra and world-renowned conductors and artists. As an entertainment center, Orchestra Hall presents the world's greatest virtuosos and ensembles in recital, America's leading jazz musicians, pop artists, operetta, and showcases of music and dance from other countries.

Another pamplet states:

Orchestra Hall is actually two buildings. The rectangular auditorium, made of concrete, brick, and oak, is isolated from all sources of mechanical and environmental noise. It is placed at a ten-degree angle on the site, and is separated from the supporting structure, which surrounds it on three sides, by a one-inch space. The supporting structure, constructed of glass, steel, and aluminum, houses the lobby and artistic and administrative offices.

The huge cubes which cover the auditorium's ceiling and front wall have become an internationally recognized trademark. If you stare at them just right, they seem to turn inside out. The cubes, which are made of plaster and set in a random pattern on a sloping surface, were designed to disperse sound throughout the hall by providing hundreds of surfaces to reflect soundwaves. White oak panels are used on most surfaces to provide a hard sound-reflecting surface. Brass screws are irregularly placed to eliminate vibration patterns. Chair backs and arms as well as most floors are made of hardwood. There is very little fabric used in the auditorium, only chair seats and aisle carpet. The lobbies and the passage surrounding the auditorium on three sides buffer street noises, aided in the winter by the coats stored in the passage lockers.

Hours: Usual concert hours **Phone**: 371-5656 **Parking**: Adjacent ramp connected by skyway **Admission**: Ranging from $6.75 to $42.50 depending on age, seat, and artist **Address**: 1111 Nicollet Mall, Minneapolis 55403 (three blocks south of the 57-story blue glass IDS tower)

The Old Log Theater

The Old Log. It's the oldest continuously running professional theater in the United States. Except for the gas rationing war years when its offerings had to be slim, it has maintained a full schedule of theater all year round since. It started on May 31, 1940, when a group of people in the neighborhood decided to organize a company to produce summer stock.

One of them donated an old log stable. That simple. By 1960 it needed many times as much space so a new Old Log was built beside the old Old Log. It has everything a theater could need: several hundred comfortable seats with good visibility and acoustics, a fine restaurant and bar, all very rustic, all very modern, a spacious lobby, and wooded outdoor rambles at intermissions.

But central to the Old Log, its personality, its inspiration, is Don Stolz, its owner, its second director, often its leading man, and as occasion demands, its ticket taker: a delightful man of many parts whose self-deprecating humor is part of his usual personal prologue before each performance. More and more, he is being supported, a little supplanted, by his sons, theatrical geniuses in their own right.

If there is a specialty, it is light comedy, English-style. The audience is usually smiling. But there are dramas and well-known Broadway titles. It has staged *Arsenic and Old Lace, Front Page, The Philadelphia Story, Life With Father, Blythe Spirit, Waiting for Godot, Charlie's Aunt, Streetcar Named Desire,* and a remarkable one-man show, *The Gospel According to St. Mark,* for the last four years as part of its Lenten series.

Hours: Usual theater hours **Phone**: 474-5951 **Parking**: Ample on site **Admission**: Usual theater prices **Address**: Box 250, Excelsior 55331 or 4175 Meadville St., Greenwood (about a mile north of Excelsior on Minnetonka Boulevard, west side of the road)

The Chanhassan Dinner Theaters

The sleepy little village of Chanhassan would seem a most unlikely host to the largest privately owned dinner theater in Minnesota. It is. It all began when Herbert Bloomberg, a contractor, was asked to build a theater for Don Stolz, founder of the Old Log Theater*. At the same time, Mr. Bloomberg, who was running out of land to develop in Edina, purchased some property on Lotus Lake, so named because it is one of only three lakes in the United States on which lotus grows wild. At the same time, he moved his business operations to Chanhassan, just south of Lotus Lake.

But the theater bug had bitten him and, hearing that a different kind of theater restaurant was becoming nation-

---

*   See Index or Contents for separate article on this topic.

ally popular, he opened the Chanhassan Dinner Theater, then called "The Frontier," in 1968. The going was tough; not until the surprise hit *Flea in Her Ear* opened in 1970 to large audiences did the operation move into the black, where it has remained. So much so that it has added three other smaller theaters, totaling 540 additional places. Every week, more than 6,000 guests are served during thirty-one performances in the quartet of theaters.

The problem with many dinner theaters has been that they think they can put on a good play and incidentally serve mediocre food, or that they can serve good food and put on a mediocre play. The Chanhassan Dinner Theater's discovery has been that a quality meal and a quality play will bring in quality money. It stresses that what happens during the dinner hours will greatly affect how the audience reacts to the play. It has 130 part-time employees and a core of 125 full-time to whom it pays good salaries with long-term contracts, both contrary to the trend.

The main theater seats 600 for dinner and the play. It puts on such plays as *Oklahoma, I do, I do, Hello Dolly, 42nd Street, My Fair Lady, Fiddler on the Roof,* and *The Mystery of Edwin Drood,* all well received.

The theater building itself, in the midst of a huge parking area, is an interesting, low, rustic style. You almost expect a hitching post. The interior, very modern but with the rustic decor, wanders. There are hallways going off in several directions, some leading to narrow stairways, some to descending ramps. Behind-the-stage tours are possible for groups.

Hours: Usual theater hours **Phone**: 934-1558 **Parking**: Ample **Admission**: Usual theater prices **Address**: Chanhassan, near intersection of State Highways 5 and 101 in the southwest corner of the metro area

The Music Box Theater

The Music Box is an intimate 300-seat theater surrounded by restaurants. The lobby is friendly. The decor is comfortable, recently redone. The tiers of seats are a little higher between each other than most so there is no trouble seeing over the people in front. The acoustics are excellent, though modern shows seem always compelled to use amplifiers.

The shows are light or musical or both. One long-running performance, *The All-Night Strut*, featured four people in numerous configurations singing dozens of songs from the thirties and forties backed by a vigorous six-piece band. The full house audience applauded vigorously at every opportunity. Afterwards, the cast came out into the lobby and discussed the play with the audience. Delightful.

The theater was built about seventy-five years ago as the Loring, a neighborhood movie house. It did well in an upscale neighborhood until the neighborhood slowly slid down-scale after World War II, aided and abetted by the invasion of television and the VCR. It was renovated as a legitimate stage, the Cricket Theater*, appealing to a larger audience. Recently its neighborhood was rejuvenated, excellent restaurants came in, and the theater was redone and converted to the Music Box. It also formed a partnership with the Chanhassen Dinner Theater*, sharing Michael Brindisi as director and collaborating on productions. It has had considerable success.

The Hyatt-Regency and the Park Inn are a block away. Pings next door serves excellent Chinese. The Brasserie across the street serves real French cooking with the ex-

---

*   See Index or Contents for separate article on this topic.

pected ambiance and service. There is an Italian restaurant, Mama Mia's, across the street and three more Italian restaurants within two blocks. Jerusalem's, next to Mama Mia's, has been voted the best Middle Eastern restaurant for five years in a row. There is a good Japanese restaurant across from the Hyatt, a sports restaurant, a magnificent steak house, and an Italian and an American restaurant in the Hyatt. Three or four blocks away there is Brits, a popular British pub, also a bagel place, the delightful Times bar, and a Thai restaurant. They complement the Music Box and it complements them, all the ingredients for a great evening.

Hours: Usually 8 p.m. **Phone**: 871-1414 **Parking**: Ramp nearby **Admission**: About $17.00 **Address**: 1407 Nicollet, Minneapolis 55403

The Children's Theater

Mention the Children's Theater and many people have visions of a theater filled with smiling, wriggling moppets, wide-eyed and excited, watching some wonderful story come to life before them. Not quite right. Statistics have shown that about 55 percent of the audience at Children's Theater performances are adults and half of those are grandparents. Some are singles, of course, and some couples, but most are adults with a child. The 20,000 performances included in season subscribers demonstrate that the Children's Theater is enthusiastically accepted by all ages, though it plays only the stories that children love . . . and adults remember.

The Moppet Players began life in 1961; in 1965 they became the Children's Theater. Since 1974 its home has been in a new 746-seat theater designed for it by Kenzo Tange as a part of the campus of the expanded Minneapolis

Art Institute* and the adjacent Minneapolis College of Art & Design. Its proscenium arch, classic wings and fly loft, computerized sound, digital lighting, and wide aisles make it a delight to visit and easy to enjoy.

In keeping with its belief that early experience with the arts can profoundly affect a child's future interest in the cultural well-being of the community, the theater presents more than 350 performances annually, reaching more than 250,000 people. Some 70,000 students and teachers attend its performances, the largest American theater for children.

The theater company also travels by chartered bus to over fifty towns in some fifteen states plus having annual artistic exchanges with youth theaters in both Russia and China.

Hours: Tuesday-Friday 7:30; Saturday 11:00, 2:00, and 7:30; Sunday 2:00 and 5:00 **Phone:** 874-0400 **Parking**: Ample in ramp **Admission**: Adults $14-$21, children $11-$16 with a 15% discount for subscribers **Address**: 2400 3rd Ave. S., Minneapolis 55404 (part of the Minneapolis Institute of Arts* campus)

The Theater in the Round Players

It was founded in 1952, making it the oldest community theater in the Twin Cities. Its unique arrangement allows for a center stage completely surrounded by 261 seats; no seat is more than thirty feet from center stage.

Differing from most theaters, Theater in the Round Players has no resident director. Rather, professionals are contracted for each production and have complete artistic control. The theater operates on a year-round basis. Around

---

*   See Index or Contents for separate article on this topic.

five hundred people are involved, contributing their time and talent in backstage work, acting, production, and support roles.

Eight plays are produced annually, everything from Shakespeare's *King Lear* to Inge's *Come Back, Little Sheba,* Graham Greene's comic *Travels with My Aunt,* mixed with farces and Tony Award Broadway plays, a rich menu.

Theater in the Round Players is managed by a volunteer board of directors elected by the membership with a paid staff of three. Plays are chosen by a committee from the community. Each season is purposefully eclectic, including classics and Broadway favorites along with area premieres such as *Equus, Great White Hope, Little Murders,* and others. George Bernard Shaw is the most popular playwright; twenty of his plays have been produced.

TRP offers workshops in acting, voice, and other skills. Auditions are open to anyone; usually eighty or so appear monthly.

Its mission is to be a premier community theater providing good entertainment and disciplined, nurturing opportunities for avocational artists, technicians, and aspiring professionals.

Hours: Friday and Saturday 8:00, Sunday 7:00 **Phone**: 333-3010 **Parking**: Curbside and ramps **Admission**: $11.00 **Address**: 245 Cedar Avenue, Minneapolis 55454 (near the West Bank Campus)

The F. Scott Fitzgerald Theatre

First it was the Schubert Theatre, built in 1910 by Sam Schubert for shows touring his Schubert circuit. In 1933 it became the World Theater because the legitimate stage could no longer compete with movies. Now, since 1994, it has been the Fitzgerald Theatre, in honor of St. Paul's great author F. Scott Fitzgerald, who is greatly admired by Garrison Keillor, the current tenant.

It was built for $165,000, made of concrete and steel with a sandstone front and sixteen dressing rooms. The stage could be lowered two feet. It had a built-in vacuum-cleaning system. It was at the cutting edge with 2,000 electric light bulbs and a side entrance for people arriving in automobiles so they wouldn't have to face a derogatory public. The *St. Paul Pioneer Press* greeted it by saying that, "It really is a beautiful playhouse because of the rich simplicity of the interior decorations, the seats being upholstered in heavy, rose-shaded plush to harmonize with the tapestry of the boxes and walls."

The theater came on hard times because the public seemed only to want comedy. The Women's City Club of St. Paul renovated it with bright colors, but even well-played Broadway shows couldn't revive it. In 1933 with another renovation, this time in the art deco manner, and another grand opening it became the World Theater, a movie house, specializing in foreign films and thus drawing audiences from a larger area. That, too, couldn't last, and in 1978 it was slated for demolition.

Coincidentally, *The Prairie Home Companion* had outgrown its place in the St. Paul-Ramsey Arts and Science Center. So MPR, Minnesota Public Radio, its mentor, leased the theater quite reasonably. In 1985 wear and tear and old age had made the building unsafe. An area-wide fund drive raised nearly two million dollars, with support from most other theater and arts organizations in the Twin Cities. Major restructuring caused it to be closed for a time and then to have yet another grand opening.

Garrison Keillor, the philosopher from Lake Wobegon and father-confessor of *The Prairie Home Companion*, is a confirmed fan of F. Scott Fitzgerald, who will continue to preside over the theater's nationally known prime tenant.

Hours: Varies with different productions **Phone**: 290-1532 **Parking**: In area **Admission**: Varies with production **Address**: Wabasha and Exchange Streets, St. Paul 55101 (near the Science Museum)

The Historic State and Orpheum Theaters

In 1921, when they opened, they were considered the finest theaters in Minnesota, certainly in Minneapolis. The State Theater is now fully restored as The Historic State Theater. A block away and equally glamorous is the restoration of The Historic Orpheum Theater.

When they initially opened, for forty-seven cents you could have the best seat in the house to see the Marx Brothers.

The Orpheum was billed as the largest vaudeville house in America, and the State was known as the most elaborate and best planned presentation house between Chicago and San Francisco. The Lyric was a block to the north, and the Pantages, now the Mann, was across the street from it. The Schubert was a half block west on Seventh and the Garrick a half block east. It made for quite a "white way."

The State and Orpheum started with vaudeville: the traveling magicians and jugglers, the dog shows and singers, the slapstick, the acrobats, rope twirlers, and comedians. The Orpheum featured such artists as Jack Benny, George Jessel, George Burns and Gracie Allen, and Fanny Brice, with day care for kids. There were cards on each end of the stage announcing the act. In the posher presentations, a master of ceremonies, always in formal black clothes, would announce each act with a buildup of superlatives.

Then came silent movies, jerky at first and with very bad camera work by today's standards. But the actors moved! It was better than staying at home with the stereopticon. Sometimes there was an orchestra in the pit to play music that was appropriate to the action on the screen. The *William Tell Overture* got a lot of use, as did bits of Strauss. There were lines along the bottom of the screen with the actors' words, as in some of the more modern opera presentations now. The actors emoted heavily enough that their meanings were usually clear without the subscripts. Horse operas were popular, as were the ones in which the villain foreclosed the mortgage because the heroine wouldn't yield to him. The hero always came in the nick of time with the money. The Villain often tied the pretty maiden to the railroad tracks and the heroe madly raced to cut her loose just as the train was about to chop her into thirds. The camera would shift from the approaching train to the approaching hero to the approaching train, back and forth. The audience applauded or booed or hissed or cried.

There were serials, the "cliff hangers," an episode every week for ten or twelve weeks, each episode ending with the hero hanging helplessly from a tree root over the edge of a cliff or in some other predicament equally impossible of rescue . . . from which he was rescued at the beginning of the next episode.

Charlie Chaplin was very much in vogue and maybe better in the silents where body language was all there was. Tom Mix wore a white hat, therefore he was a good guy. Big stars were never bad guys. Harold Lloyd did his own comic urban cliff-hanging. Buster Keaton did his deadpan comedies. Laurel and Hardy were as good without sound. The greatest of the silents though was *Birth of a Nation*, an epic of the aftermath of the Civil War, surprisingly candid about racial conditions and the Ku Klux Klan. It was long. By today's standards, the photography was terrible and the actors all hams, but it was the best photography available and they had to ham because they couldn't talk. Try telling somebody something without your voice. It won whatever prizes there were to win.

"Talkies" came in the late twenties, like a miracle. Radios were just becoming common. Blessed air-conditioning arrived in the thirties, in the theaters before anywhere else. People went to the movies just to get out of the heat. With the Depression came "Bank Night" where the ticket stub number was used for prizes of food or money, sometimes as much as ten dollars. There were musicals—*Forty Second Street, The Ziegfield Follies*—with much dancing, a love affair, a debonair older man, an ingenue, always with a bright and happy ending to counteract the Depression's depressions. When *Lilac Time* came to the State, the lobby and much of the auditorium were filled with lilacs. It smelled great.

But with television the theaters were abandoned, both of them. For some years the State was a sedate religious meeting house, then abandoned again, old newspapers blowing into its entry, its marquee disheveled. The Orpheum sat empty. It was repainted and some shows brought in 1979 and again in 1984, but it was falling into disrepair. In 1988 major items were fixed, but it was still an old theater.

Then came the great restorations of 1991—about $9 million of renovation for each building. The State's interior again became exactly the same, elegant, Italian Renaissance. Murals were repainted. The crystal chandeliers were rebuilt. The cherubs came back. The gilt was carefully replaced. New carpets were laid. The crimsons and blues were strikingly repainted. The great curtain once again slid open with dignity. A dazzling marquee was installed, brightening up the avenue. Its name was changed to the Historic State Theater.

The bigger Orpheum was totally redone, its stage extended back to be large enough for the 747 in *Miss Saigon*. New dressing rooms were added and new mechanical equipment installed. A sign of the times was the considerable enlargement of the number of ladies' restrooms.

But instead of Hollywood's tinsel, now they brought the best of live entertainment to the Twin Cities, and the Twin Cities responded with full houses, all 2,100 newly upholstered seats of the State and 2,600 of the Orpheum. Evening business downtown has boomed with the new crowds and new restaurants. A $2 restoration fee added to each ticket is repaying all costs on schedule.

Hours: Usual theater times. **Phone**: 339-7007 **Parking**: Ramps in area **Admission**: Usual major theater prices **Addresses**: The Historic State Theater is at 805 Hennepin, Minneapolis 55403 (two blocks west of the IDS Tower). The Historic Orpheum Theater is a block south and across the street with the same phone number.

The Dudley Riggs' Theaters

With such marvelous show titles as *The Vice Man Cometh, I Compute Therefore IBM, The Censorship of Fools or Jesse at the Helm, Aging Bull or Sex and the Senior Citizen,* or *National Velvet or What a Friend We have in Cheeses*, it is no wonder that Dudley Riggs' Brave New Workshop is alive and doing very well after thirty-five years.

Dudley Riggs, the founder, is the fifth generation of a vigorous show business family. From age five he has worked as a comedian, aerialist, writer, stage director, and whatever. In the late 1950s he founded the Instant Theater in New York City. Opening off-Broadway, the show consisted of sketches and burlesque with much input from the audience.

The new innovation was hugely successful if only because each new show was different and no scene ever quite anticipated.

After touring nationally, a permanent home was found in the Twin Cities in 1961 as The Brave New Workshop. A sideline was to provide customized shows for corporations and educational classes. In 1971 he founded the Experimental Theater Company with a cafe at Seven Corners next to the West Bank Campus of the University.

National Public Radio's "All Things Considered" named The Brave New Workshop its resident satire company, and in 1992 KTCA public television produced an hour-long program entitled "Dudley Riggs American Scream." In 1984 he received the fourth annual Urban Guerrilla Award by the committee dedicated to the Concept of a Universal Humanistic Future.

Approximately three million people have been "exposed to" the performance of over two hundred and fifty productions; four hundred college campuses in over forty states have been visited and there have been USO tours in Europe. There have been some five hundred actors and comedians, including Louie Anderson, John Cada, Tom Davis, Al Franken, Pat Proft, Gary Rayppy, and Susan Vass. Writers who have also succeeded are Mike Anthony, Doris Hess, Peggy Knapp, Irv Letofsky, Nancy Steen, and Peter Tolan, among many others. Writers have gone on to write, perform, and produce for such television programs as "Mash," "The Mary Tyler Moore Show," "Webster," "Murphy Brown," and "Saturday Night Live." Film work includes *Poltergeist*, *Sophie's Choice*, *Airplane*, *Ruthless People*, *Police Academy*, and *Naked Gun*.

With thirty-five exciting years behind him, Dudley Riggs' goals in the next thirty-five years are to "expand local and national touring, have a syndicated commercial radio program, a live interactive television show, more youth education programs, and finally a larger, more accessible base of operations."

The future? In his own titles, *Don't Worry, Be Stupid, Yuppie See, Yuppie Do*. His public will never stop chuckling.

Hours: Usual theater times **Phone**: 332-6620 **Parking**: Curbside **Admission**: Usual theater charges **Address**: 2605 Hennepin, Minneapolis 55408 (four blocks north of "Uptown," about three miles south of the river)

The Penumbra Theater

The following is from literature about the Penumbra:

The Penumbra Theater Company, resident theater company of the Hallie Q. Brown Community Center, was founded in 1976 by Artistic Director, Lou Bellamy. Under his continuous leadership Penumbra has added an important dimension of cultural experience to the Community Center and the Upper Midwest region. In addition, Penumbra has larger challenges, to provide a much needed performance vehicle for the Twin Cities artistic community, as well as employ more African American administrators, directors, designers, playwrights, and performing artists than any other theater arts organization in Minnesota.

Balancing the pursuit of artistic excellence in productions with the African American interests of Penumbra and the surrounding community has presented some unique challenges. The solution has been a mix of entertainment and education opportunity presented in the community, and for the community at large. As a result, Penumbra takes deliberate risks in choosing the plays for production.

The subject matter is often about the immediate community. As a community based theater, Penumbra is committed to the people of that community as well as the performing and literary arts of the community at large. This commitment is vividly illustrated through the work produced on the mainstage, as well as such programs as *Understudy and Training Program* and *Summer Institute* [programs for high school and college age members of the community to study and work with company members], as well as the *Cornerstone Competition* [a national playwriting competition].

. . . Penumbra [also] provides an important modeling and education function for members of its community. Through the introduction of young actors, musicians, and technicians, their subsequent development at Penumbra, artists of exceptional quality have and will continue to secure positions in many of the area's and nation's theaters. Some of these artists are now making significant and important contributions to the artistic community, locally and nationally.

As a forum for the playwrights who strive to present alternatives to the majority view, Penumbra's Cornerstone Competition provides the perfect blend of exciting talent and artistic support found few places across the nation. The competition winner, selected by the committee, is awarded a cash prize, an in-residence workshop of the winning entry with company members and the Playwrights' Center, and the [mainstage] production of the winning entry."

Hours: Usual theater hours **Phone**: 224-7074 **Parking**: Curbside **Admission**: About $17-$23 for adults, depending on the date; about $12-$17 for seniors and students. **Address**: 270 N. Kent, St. Paul 55102

Theatre de la Jeune Lune

The seats can be moved to fit the play: with the stage against the high blank wall on one side of the room, or against the windows on the other side, or in a theater-in-the-round configuration. The ceiling is forty feet high, allowing dramatic use of sheer space to emphasize the scene. The stage can be wide or narrow, vertical or low. The theater, even the audience, can be arranged to fit the play instead of having to tune the play to a fixed theater.

It's what happens when you move to a warehouse, a cavernous warehouse. The options are greatly expanded, but so are the problems. Space eats up sound, so actors have constantly to project their voices to the rear seats to be heard. Bigger space allows bigger sets, which can be a nightmare for the set designers, and the bigger space may have to be overcome for plays that call for a feeling of intimacy.

Vincent Gracieux, the co-artistic director, enjoys the challenge. He's perfectly comfortable changing the audience chairs if it will enhance the performance, or changing the set dimensions, or using up all the height. In *Germinal*, he brought in huge pieces of construction equipment to dominate the empty, torn-up ground of a small village in France. For *Burial*, he transplanted twenty-five-foot trees to the stage. For *The Green Bird*, he had to go the other way, the drama playing best in a small setting.

The Theatre de la Jeune Lune is in its second decade. In that time it has done a lot of moving itself, at the Hennepin Center for the Arts*, which has birthed many artistic ventures, at the Southern Theater, which has been used for many types of performances, and at the Guthrie's* Labora-

---

*   See Index or Contents for separate article on this topic.

tory in the Warehouse District*, which was designed to assist problems such as the "Loonies" often face.

It is an international theater company. It has created its own productions, it has done its own interpretations of the classics, it has commissioned new scripts. It likes large issues and large casts but it can adapt to small issues and small casts. Its most recent presentations have been a comedy, *Conversations after a Burial,* highly thought of in France; *Don Juan Don Giovanni,* a theme Mozart and Moliere used; *The Juniper Tree,* a play for families using both live and puppet actors; and *Pelleas and Melisande,* Maeterlinck's story of a medieval love affair between a wife and her half-brother, done as an opera by Debussy and adapted by Hollywood some years ago.

(Background data for the preceding was provided by the *Star Tribune.*)

Hours: Thursday-Saturday 8:00, Sunday 7:00 Some mornings and some matinees **Phone**: 333-6200 **Parking**: Ramps and lots **Admission**: Adults $7-$14, discounts for seniors, students, and groups **Address**: 105 First Street North, Minneapolis 55401 (a block north of Washington Avenue, a block west of Hennepin)

---

*   See Index or Contents for separate article on this topic.

CHAPTER 9

Interesting People

Hubert Humphrey

Hubert Horatio Humphrey left his drug store in South Dakota and came to Minneapolis, and the city and the state have never been quite the same. He became mayor of Minneapolis and used it as a bully pulpit. He also used it for the good of the city.

Most everyone in the city at the time agreed that the Lower Loop should be torn down. It was a blight. It was a skid row. It was valuable property. It once had been Bridge Square where the city had begun, then its commercial center. Later it had been the Gateway, to signify that the commercial center had moved south along Nicollet. There was even a classical arch erected at the foot of Nicollet, where it met Hennepin. But then it deteriorated. It became the Lower Loop, well known as a place for bums and drunks. Demolishing it would cost more money than the city could afford. The federal government said it would put up the money if the city would build one significant building in the area as a starter. Heads were scratched until Mayor Humphrey also realized that the city had outgrown its lovely old library on Tenth Street. So he put the package together and

Minneapolis got a nice new library and got rid of a tired piece of its history.

In the process, under the capable direction of Bob Jorvig, a survey was made of the denizens of the skid row. It was found that there were 1,006 permanent residents, over 99 percent older males, almost all living on their railroad pensions or Social Security. Over 40 percent were alcoholics, on the basis that anyone who regularly had more than one drink a day of anything was an alcoholic! It had a very low crime rate except for prostitution and public drunkenness by persons who lived elsewhere. And it was found that a woman was totally safe on its streets at any hour, the men remembering a mother, a sister, or a wife whom they held in special regard.

Minnesota was essentially a Republican state. There was a Democratic Party. There was a small Labor Party—Minneapolis was a hotbed of organized labor, especially the Teamsters who physically took over downtown in their 1934 strike—and there was a small Farmers Party. But the three mostly fought each other and let Republicans win the elections. Mayor Humphrey changed this. With help from, among many others, Walter Mondale, who later became vice president, Orville Freeman who later became governor and Secretary of Agriculture, Arthur Naftalin who later became mayor and an excellent Commissioner of Administration, he organized the Democratic-Farmer-Labor Party (DFL) in the late 1940s. It took over the state and continues to have a lock on the Legislature, the urban county boards, and the Twin Cities.

He was everywhere. His smile was a part of the landscape. You might disagree with his liberal views, but you'd like him as a person; it was a pleasure to be around him. If there had been television, he would have dominated the six o'clock and ten o'clock news every day.

He went on to Washington as a United States Senator and quickly established himself as the prime liberal. For a while some other liberals weren't sure they wanted to be seen with him, but then he became their leader and remained so. He was proffered the keynote speech at the Democratic National Convention, a place of high honor, and gave not just a speech but an oration on Civil Rights, so powerful that it forced the country to move it to the fore of its politics as the touchstone of "political correctness."

He served as vice president of the United States under Lyndon Johnson. In 1968, in a wild convention in Chicago, he was nominated as the Democratic candidate for president of the United States of America. But he was tarred with Johnson's expansion of the Vietnam War and was defeated by Richard Nixon.

He was returned to his seat in the Senate and served there until his second and last defeat, by cancer. He was succeeded in the Senate by his wife, Muriel, who was Minnesota's first female senator.

He is remembered with affection by tens of thousands of his fellow citizens. The international terminal of the airport has been named for him, as has the huge Metrodome Stadium, the site of so many national sports contests. At the south entrance to the Minneapolis Courthouse*, there is a lifelike statue of him. He is speaking and looking very convincing; unfortunately the statue is rather overwhelmed by the massive entrance around it. Best of all the remembrances dedicated to this dynamic man is the Hubert Humphrey Institute, a think tank graduate school at the University of Minnesota which attracts many great minds.

---

* See Index or Contents for separate article on this topic.

If Al Smith had not already claimed it, Hubert Humphrey would surely merit the title of "The Happy Warrior."

Bud Grant

He was "Most Valuable Player" in baseball and was a sought-after pitcher who made more money on one-night stands than the pros were making with their season contracts. He was "Most Valuable Player" in basketball and played defense with George Mikan and Jim Pollard on the championship Minneapolis Lakers before they were transferred to Los Angeles. In the Navy, he played football for Great Lakes and beat Notre Dame. He played Canadian football and made the Canadian Pro Bowl. He coached pro football and made the National Football League Hall of Fame in Canton, Ohio. All this despite not having enough food for seconds as he was growing up and polio at age eight that left his left calf and thigh smaller than his right and required lifts in his shoe.

He coached his Vikings to ten conference championships and four Superbowls. He was the highest paid coach in professional football. He was never fired but he retired twice. He is a legend in Minnesota. It was comforting to see him standing on the sidelines during a game, never a change of expression, never excited, never exuberant, never depressed. He was a stoic. He was an excellent coach, maybe because he put his own family and kids ahead of his job.

And he did it all his way. On his terms. At his times.

F. Scott Fitzgerald

Francis Scott Key Fitzgerald, named after the author of the *Star Spangled Banner*, an ancestor on his paternal side, was born in St. Paul in 1896. His mother was of a well-to-do family so he was able to attend St. Paul Academy (an outstanding prep school), Newman School, and Princeton University. He was always "tantalizingly close," but never quite a part of his contemporaries of great wealth and position, which is evident in many of his novels. Maybe the irony is that his fame has outlived all of theirs.

He left Princeton without a degree in 1917 and served in the army during World War I and until 1919. His experience made him say, "I wasn't on the football team at Princeton and was never sent overseas by the Army;" both were great disappointments to a very vibrant, strange young man.

F. Scott Fitzgerald, one of the great writers of his time and about his time, called his works "part of the Jazz Age." As he described it, he was part of "a new generation grown up to find all gods dead, all wars fought, all faiths in man shaken." His characters lead a life of never-ending fun, endless parties, and much wealth, yet he seems to be seeking something real other than the fantasy they are all living.

His novel *This Side of Paradise* was started when he was in the army. Published in 1920, it is autobiographical and part of the revolt of rebellious youth. The same year he married Zelda Sayre, a beautiful daughter of an Alabama judge, and they led what many would consider a gilded life. They traveled to fashionable resorts in Europe, lived in Paris, New York, Long Island, and Washington; all of these amidst splendor akin to his novels. He published many short stories and then *The Great Gatsby*, one of his finest works, followed by more short stories.

Time and excessive living did bring dreadful emotional and financial pressures. Zelda became a victim of an incurable mental illness, requiring Fitzgerald to write magazine articles to cover the costs of her care. Despite these demands he was able to write *Tender is the Night.* His own health began deteriorating. He tried to put his life back together and wrote his final novel, *The Last Tycoon,* one of his best.

In 1994, a half century after his death in 1940, he received an interesting recognition: At the behest of one of his great admirers, Garrison Keillor*, the theater which has been the home of *The Prairie Home Companion* with appropriate fanfare has been renamed the F. Scott Fitzgerald*.

Sinclair Lewis

He wrote much and cuttingly about the "Babbitts," the businessmen whose base of operations was the Minneapolis Athletic Club, where they pontificated shallowly and vowed never to join the Minneapolis Club down the street where the economic rulers of the city belonged—unless they were asked. He also wrote about the provincialism and the smugness of American small towns based on his recollections of Sauk Centre in northwestern Minnesota where he grew up. He called it "Gopher Prairie," the gopher being the official Minnesota state animal and northwestern Minnesota being flat, and titled his 1920 book *Main Street.* It was not well received on Main Street, but it was a national success in the postwar years—his first success as a novelist—and was read as a best seller for several decades.

---

*   See Index or Contents for separate article on this topic.

He was born in Sauk Centre in 1885. During his youth he was awkward, introspective, and lonely, with few friends. He graduated from Yale in 1908. He worked as a reporter and in an editorial capacity for several publishing houses. He also wrote prolifically for magazines, becoming widely known.

Always concerned about social problems, he followed with *Babbitt,* probably his greatest work, about a complacent man who loses his individuality by conforming too well with the norms of his peers. In 1925 he wrote *Arrowsmith*, a satire on the medical profession and its frustrations. *Elmer Gantry* was an exposure of unsavory elements of the Protestant church who were more interested in self-aggrandizement than the Gospel. *Dodsworth* concerns an American automobile maker and his wife in Europe, emphasizing the contrasting values of Europe and America of that day.

After being awarded the Nobel prize in 1930, his work declined and he seemed to lose his vitriolic, satirical attitudes.

His best work in the '30s, during the rise of Hitler, was *It Can't Happen Here,* in which he demonstrates quite logically how a Hitler could come to power in the United States without destroying any democratic niceties. It fitted so well into what the newspapers were reporting that many Americans, complacent behind their oceans from the problems of Asia and Europe, began to realize that they were part of the world out there.

The two most important books of his later life were *Cass Timberlane*, about an older man and his young wife, and *Kingsblood Royal*, a story about race relations.

While not all of his critics agree about his importance in literature, they all admit that his style was vigorous, effective, and led to social consciousness by many Americans. His books contain much disguised biography of himself.

He deplored the Babbitts—and he loved them.

The Twins

In 1961 the Washington Senators became the Minnesota Twins. The previous teams had used more customary names: the St. Paul Saints, the Minneapolis Millers. When the major leagues hove in sight, both cities went after a team, and both proposed to build the necessary large stadium; the cities were very competitive. Just as they had a generation earlier when it was decided that the metropolitan airport could be built anywhere in the state that was equidistant from both city halls, so it was decided to build the stadium equidistant, near the airport which is required by law to be equidistant, and call the team the *Minnesota* Twins to satisfy, or dissatisfy, both cities equally.

It was a great day when they arrived. The Twin Cities had become major league! We were on the map! The problem was that, when they arrived, very few residents knew much about major league baseball. Our main contact had been when we were both farm teams and the majors stole players just as they got good. Now suddenly these were our players, but we didn't know their names.

We learned quickly, and proudly. Harmon Killebrew, a sweet guy who loved children and could hit home runs quite frequently, made such an impression that a street was named after him. Then there was Tony Oliva, with the big smile, a great shortstop with a big bat, and Rod Carew whom everyone liked. It was great to be in the majors, even if the population was smaller than most so that there was less TV money and thus other teams could hire our players away with higher salaries. Calvin Griffith, the owner, countered that by developing the best farm system and bringing on great new players.

Two more big names came with the years. Kent Hrbek had grown up living a mile or two from Met Stadium and always dreamed of playing in it. He became a great first baseman but was denied his final triumph when the 1994 baseball strike ended all play for the year, leaving him with an incomplete final season as he was on the way to records.

Kirby Puckett, like the flashlight battery, goes on and on and on, making the fans happier and happier and happier with his dramatic catches and agile bat. His playing skill is well-known; what he has done for his community, for kids, and for his family is not as well-known, nor apparently does he want it to be.

Fish Jones

He stood five feet five inches, so he always wore an eight-inch top hat. To fit the top hat he always wore a long Prince Albert dress coat and suitable shirts and cravats. He always wore a full, carefully trimmed beard. He walked with great dignity, looking neither left nor right, often with a pair of magnificent Russian wolfhounds. That he sold fish was usually apparent from several yards away. A wonderful, colorful character, he was widely known as "Fish Jones."

He came from New York in 1876 and opened a fish market on Bridge Square, then the center of all commercial activity. He was the first vendor to sell oysters in Minneapolis. For publicity, he acquired a pet seal who roamed around the store. He also acquired a carriage once owned by the Grand Duke Alexis of Russia and had it drawn by two pairs of black and gray horses, at one time being accompanied in his carriage by General William Tecumseh Sherman and at another by former President Ulysses S. Grant.

His interest in horses and animals prompted him to buy a farm out in the country, where the Basilica* now stands, across the Sculpture Garden* from the Walker Art Center*. He bought Dan Patch, one of the greatest horses of all times, a pacer who in 1905 set a world record 1:55 quarter mile that stood for sixty years.

He was a great admirer of Henry Wadsworth Longfellow so he had a house built that was an exact replica of Longfellow's home in Cambridge, Massachusetts. Both houses still stand. Fish Jones—he was always known as "Fish"—built his house on Minnehaha Creek, just above the falls where there is a statue of Hiawatha carrying Minnehaha across the stream, just as Longfellow wrote in "The Song of Hiawatha." The house was beautiful but he added a zoo in its yard. It was the best zoo in the Twin Cities in 1906 because it was the only one, but it was mangy and malodorous and not loved by its neighbors. Just before his death in 1930, he arranged to give the house and zoo to the Park Board who in turn closed the zoo and gave the house to the Public Library for a branch. For many years, however, there was a pony ride in the side yard where small children could ride around a rather small circle and fancy themselves cowboys.

Walter Mondale

Walter Mondale is a lucky man and an unlucky man. In the inner circle of the D.F.L., he was lucky enough to be appointed as Minnesota's Attorney General when Miles Lord became a colorful, populist, federal judge. He was

---

*   See Index or Contents for separate article on this topic.

easily elected to the position at the next election. He was lucky enough to be appointed to the United States Senate when Hubert Humphrey became vice president and again was easily elected to the position at the next election. He was lucky enough to be anointed by Jimmy Carter as vice president but then was supremely unlucky in running into the Ronald Reagan juggernaut when he ran for president. Clinton made him Ambassador to Japan, a tough assignment.

He is a good lawyer, which in his case is not an oxymoron. He is a nice guy. He is at his best in small groups where the reasonableness of his positions becomes clearest.

Harold Stassen

He was the youngest of Minnesota's governors, from 1939 to 1943, a *wunderkind* before the term had been invented. He did a remarkable job of reorganizing and modernizing state government, with reforms that are still in place. He left to go to war, serving as Admiral Halsey's Chief of Staff during the Third Fleet's continual hammering of the Japanese. He assisted in the founding of the United Nations, signing the original charter, and then became the president of the University of Pennsylvania.

He reads voraciously. He has maintained a network of well-placed friends. He talks a lot, but he also listens well. He is very much aware of the world around him and has reasonable and practical solutions for many of its problems.

He ran for president in 1948 and every four years thereafter. He'll probably run again in 1996. The country would have been much the better if he had prevailed at any or all of those times.

Floyd B. Olson

He was County Attorney of Hennepin County during the roistering days of the twenties and went on to be governor in the chaotic days of the early thirties. He loved the good life and lived it well. He had some of the characteristics of his contemporary, Huey P. Long, of Louisiana.

His most difficult moment was probably being forced to call out the National Guard to suppress a massive and violent strike by his friends, the Teamsters Union. He withheld his decision until citizens had been killed on the picket line, the police had been forced into hiding, and teamsters were directing traffic at the street corners.

He had aspirations for the United States Senate and probably for the presidency. But death came too early.

Frederick Feikema Manfred

He was a mountain of a man, a happy Finn. He became the greatest of the authors of a special genre, stories of the mountain men, those individualistic souls who roamed the Rockies in search of fur, living with and sometimes against the Indians but mostly living contentedly alone with the animals, coming together to trade their furs once a year in a wild and wonderful orgy. They were a special breed. And so was Frederick Manfred.

George Draper Dayton

In 1881 George Draper Dayton, descendant of the four-teenth century De Deightons of York, England, arrived in Worthington, Minnesota, twenty-four years old, as representative of a group of bankers from Starkey, in upstate New York. The bankers had invested money in a real estate development of an enthusiastic developer who had no administrative talents. Mr. Dayton was only five feet four inches tall but he had such a natural presence that he was automatically respected. He soon bought the local bank as an operating base and prepared to settle into this still frontier country. He straightened out the real estate development and broadened the bank's interest in building up the area.

In 1896, after studying Chicago, Denver, Kansas City, and Minneapolis, he decided that Minneapolis showed the greatest possibilities of growth. It had a population of 200,000 and was the center of large lumber, iron, and wheat enterprises as well as two international milling empires. The city had also already begun its cultural development. It was a waiting paradise for merchandising. But Mr. Dayton then was a banker and real estate agent. He moved his business and gradually became the largest landholder on Nicollet, much of it still almost rural, at a time when the city was still clinging to the river.

He was not a tall man, but he was a dignified man, with a well-trimmed beard, always conservatively dressed in the appropriate clothes of the occasion.

Westminister Presbyterian Church had built an imposing stone building on the west side of Seventh and Nicollet at the southern edge of the business district. Beyond that were houses and some farms. The church burned down, leaving a hazardous shell. The church wanted to move, but no one would buy its property because it was too far south. After nearly a year, Mr. Dayton was persuaded. He had built the six-story Dayton building at Sixth and Nicollet primarily for physicians. He planned to build a similar building at Seventh with some shops on the first level and Goodfellows, a drygoods company which he had bought when it was on Third Street. Donaldson's "Glass Block" had established itself a block closer to the river ten years before. Mr. Dayton had had no experience as a merchant and intended the new building to be primarily an office building, so Goodfellows was given only half the ground floor space in the new building, with various separately owned departments scattered through the building. One of these, Harrington Beard's Art Galleries*, was on the fourth floor; it continues today but farther south, at Tenth on the Nicollet Mall*. Dayton's grew by having a goal of being a supplier of everything to everybody at a fair price and with quality goods. Gradually his son Draper Dayton took over management and with George Nelson Dayton built the store to be the preeminent retailer in the upper Midwest states.

George Dayton was a man of uncompromising principles. He didn't try to impose them on others, but he guided his own life by them. He was a devout Christian, attending church quietly and sincerely, tithing, as well as supporting its causes. He could recite large passages of the Bible appropriate to a situation. He had total respect for the Sabbath. His children were not allowed outside to play on Sunday; he spent no money on Sunday, not even for a newspaper. He would not travel on Sunday nor permit anyone in Dayton's to travel on its business on Sunday. The store was closed and there were no advertisements in the newspapers. The street level show windows were all dark. He would not permit

---

*   See Index or Contents for separate article on this topic.

alcohol in his home or in the store, nor the glasses or housewares for serving it. But he was generous to charities and he sought out unfortunates and helped them. He contributed not just money but energy in developing Minneapolis' cultural facilities. He had an abiding faith in the young and singled them out and helped them in unique ways.

John Sargent Pillsbury

He was instrumental in ending the long delay in bringing the University of Minnesota into existence in 1869, fifteen years after Hamline was started (though Hamline, founded in Red Wing, had closed in 1869 because of problems from the war and reopened in St. Paul in 1882). Mr. Pillsbury served on the Board of Regents at the University until 1895 and became known as the "Father of the University." He became governor of Minnesota in 1876. He loaned his nephew Charles A. Pillsbury the money to create the Pillsbury Milling Company, which in 1893 built the Pillsbury "A" Mill, the largest flour mill in the world.

Both of the Pillsburys and all of their progeny supported the arts and culture of the community and influenced the strong role of Minneapolis in the affairs of the world. The third generation, also John Pillsbury, became president of the Northwestern National Life Insurance Company and, as such, built one of the most beautiful buildings in the city down by what had been Bridge Square.

Warren Burger

He looks like the Chief Justice. He acts like the Chief Justice. And from 1969 to 1986 he was the Chief Justice.

He grew up in St. Paul and attended the St. Paul College of Law which later combined with the Minneapolis College of Law to become today's well-regarded William Mitchell College of Law, one of Minnesota's three law schools, named after an early and much-respected Chief Justice of the Minnesota Supreme Court.

He was first appointed to the federal courts by President Eisenhower in 1953 and by President Nixon to be its Chief Justice in 1969. He guided the court through the often riotous Vietnam years, upholding civil rights, and through the abortion uproar. He is a man of considerable thought and of a deeply held political philosophy. Outside the court he has participated in numerous efforts to improve the nation's judiciary, notably the National Center for State Courts, which he founded. He has been often a lone voice in trying to expedite the criminal justice system.

Garrison Keillor

He wanted to be a poet when he grew up in Anoka*. Instead he brought a gentle fame to Minnesota by expounding on the virtues of *Lake Wobegon* where all the children are above average. He talked much of the ploys and idiosyncrasies of the Lutherans and the Norwegians without upset-

---

* See Index or Contents for separate article on this topic.

ting either of these two stalwart groups of Minnesotans. He loves to present the musical symposium "A Young Lutheran's Guide to the Orchestra." He has disclosed to outsiders some of the niceties of speaking "Minnesotan" ("You betcha my boots!") and taught them a little of "Minnesota Nice." He made even the iconoclasts look forward each week to another chapter of his philosophy. The tapes and books of his homilies became best-sellers. How could they not? There was a hiatus while he sampled the glories of Denmark and New York, but now he is back and with the wonderful panache of changing the name of St. Paul's World Theater to the F. Scott Fitzgerald* Theatre.

Maria Sanford

Maria Sanford was the first woman to become a full professor. She came from Swarthmore College in Pennsylvania in 1880 and taught elocution and rhetoric until 1909 at the University of Minnesota, becoming extremely popular with the students but unpopular with the faculty for her independent ways. In the nation's capitol in Washington, the former House chambers have become a Statuary Hall, with each state authorized to emplace two statues. Henry Rice* was the first chosen. In 1958 it was decided that Minnesota's second statue would be of Maria Sanford. A dormitory has been named for her on the campus.

---

* See Index or Contents for separate article on this topic.

Pierre "Pig's Eye" Parrant

"A Canadian voyageur, with a bad reputation and sinister features, by the name of Pierre Parrant, has the honor of being the first settler of our saintly city. From all accounts he was an ugly looking fellow but no doubt brave. He had an eye that resembled that of a pig, and hence the place was early called 'Pig's Eye,' which euphonious name it bore for several years. Parrant built the first log house in Saint Paul in 1838 . . . and at the close of that year nine cabins graced the future city, composed of a motley group of Canadians and Swiss French. Of course Parrant had to live, so he opened up a trade with the soldiers and Indians of poisonous whisky, and no doubt for a time both he and his fellow traders did a thriving business. I believe he subsequently moved down river about three miles to a place now called 'Pig's Eye [Island],' but what finally became of him nobody seems to know." Quoted from *Trail Explorer,* a publication of the Minnesota Department of Natural Resources, itself quoting from *Pen Pictures of Saint Paul, Minnesota, and Biographical Sketches of Old Settlers, from the Earliest Settlement of the City, Up to and including the year 1857* Volume I, by T.M. Newson, 1886.

A Pig's Eye beer has been named for Mr. Parrant and has achieved a national market. His island in the river, which is used for the metropolitan sanitation system, is also named for Pig's Eye.

Charles Schulz

In 1947 a comic strip known as "Li'l Folks" first appeared, drawn by a young Minneapolis man who had been drawing for years with no particular success, which didn't surprise him because, as he himself says, he'd flunked everything, including dating. The name of the comic strip was changed in 1950 to "Peanuts" and United Features found seven papers who would publish it as a space saver. Now it appears in 2,400 newspapers with 200 million readers in sixty-eight countries because, according to Greg Howard of Minneapolis who draws *Sally Forth,* we all know a Charlie Brown or have a little bit of Charlie in us. Most of us feel the frustrations of Sally from time to time, too.

There was a real Charlie Brown, a friend of Charlie Schulz. He was an adult but he was a Charlie Brown. He worked at the Hennepin County Juvenile Detention Center where his Charlie Brown-ish characteristics allowed him to move peacefully and effectively among the often-violent, delinquent juveniles. Maybe he would have been even more effective if he'd had a Snoopy.

Snoopy, too, has come home to the Twin Cities. In the Mall of America, the nation's largest shopping mall, Camp Snoopy is the central attraction, bringing in the kids by the thousands with their parents in tow. Kids can safely be left alone at Camp Snoopy while their parents shop.

Prince Rogers Nelson

His first name really is Prince, named by his jazz pianist father after the Prince Rogers Trio in which the father played. He bounced between divorced parents and relatives and ended up in the basement of his best friend's home with whom he organized a band, "Champagne." He was offered numerous contracts but he did what he wanted: he was his own boss, and now he has his own recording studios, "Paisley Park," in Chanhassen* in the southwest corner of the metro area. His success has been huge and justified, developing his own complex and satisfying style and numerous unpronounceable syllables.

James Arness

Matt Dillon, the strong and sagacious marshal of Dodge City on "Gunsmoke," the role model of some thousands of young males, was born in Minneapolis in 1918 in the person of James Arness. The reruns may keep his name alive for generations, a needed influence in these perilous times.

His brother, Peter Graves, known for his outstanding work in "Mission Impossible," was also born in Minneapolis, in 1926. Both possibly were precursors to the growing motion picture industry in the area.

---

*   See Index or Contents for separate article on this topic.

Sister Elizabeth Kenny

Photo courtesy of Hennepin
County Historical Society

The title is military, not religious, from her days in the Australian army; it was a promotion equivalent to chief nurse. She was proud of it. She had spent many years in the isolated Australian bush country where she had evolved her theory for treating polio by therapy rather than bed rest and pharmaceuticals. She had seen it work and work well. The usual treatment was immobilizing the affected limbs in casts or braces. She found the exact opposite worked: use hot, moist packs to relieve the muscular tightness and pain and they would become useful again. After thirty-three years of using her treatment in Australia, she came to the United States. Her reception in California was cool, so she went to New York to the National Foundation for Infantile Paralysis. Her reception in New York also was less than enthusiastic. So she headed home, stopping in Rochester's Mayo Clinic because she had letters of introduction there. Her reception in the Midwest was warm. She was given a professional audience. It was in Minneapolis hospitals where she met the soft-spoken and well-respected Dr. Miland Knapp. The doctor was quickly convinced Sister Elizabeth Kenny's unconventional methods of treatment had significant value in the rehabilitation of polio victims. In time, it was his influence and guidance that helped Sister Elizabeth Kenny overcome her abrasive manner and improve her position both professionally and personally.

Her success resulted in a twenty-two-bed ward in one hospital, then an additional seventeen-bed ward in another. News of her success spread over the country, which was enduring a polio epidemic. Patients began arriving in Minneapolis in increasing numbers, often without a reservation because they feared being turned away unless they were right on her doorstep. A program was established for teaching others. A small hospital was converted to the Elizabeth Kenny Institute. The Exchange Club underwrote a home for her near the Institute. Senator Hubert Humphrey became a sponsor and was her legislative watchdog.

Six years after she arrived in Minneapolis, a movie was made of her life starring Rosalind Russell and Cary Grant, opening to more than 20,000 people in Times Square in the New York which had rejected her. As polio was gradually erased, her Sister Kenny Institute was combined with, but never merged, with the 700-bed Abbott-Northwestern Hospital, where its name and its work in related fields proceed as Sister Kenny would have wanted. At her death, Dr. Arnold Lowe of Westminister Church eulogized:

> It is difficult to crowd a life such as Sister Elizabeth Kenny's into the compass of mere words. There was something depthless about this life; a life spurred on by divine urging and finding its boundaries in the miseries and hopes of mankind.

Henry Mower Rice

A fur trader who had an influential role in the formation of the state and its admission into the Union, Henry Mower Rice became an early United States Senator, opposing slavery and supporting the Union when both positions were contentious enough to bring on a war. A county has also been named after him.

In the capitol in Washington when the building was expanded, the old House chambers was converted to a statuary hall in which each state was entitled to place two statues. Henry Rice's statue was the first chosen, emplaced in 1916. The second was of Maria Sanford*.

Father Galtier

The Reverend Lucian Galtier was a Catholic priest who in 1841 built the Chapel of St. Paul in a town known as Pig's Eye after Mr. Pierre Parrant*, its first settler. Though it was the very first church building for white settlers in Minnesota, it wasn't much; Father Galtier described it as about on a par with the stable at Bethlehem. The chapel became the focus of the town. At the behest of the father the powers that were decided that St. Paul was a more dignified name. If they had not, the capital of Minnesota would be Pig's Eye, which would have been a name of renown.

A plaza has been named for the good father in the center of St. Paul with some fine high-rise buildings; a nationally marketed beer and an island in the Mississippi River have been named for Mr. Parrant.

---

*   See Index or Contents for separate article on this topic.

Martin McLeod

A Canadian fur trader who liked books, he sponsored a bill in 1849 that created free schools open to all persons between the ages of four and twenty-one. The schools were only open three months a year and basically taught only reading and writing, but they were schools nevertheless, and Minnesota became the first state to adopt universal free education. A county was named for McLeod.

William Folwell

At thirty-four years of age in 1869, he became the first president of the University of Minnesota. Where now there are about 50,000 students, there were then 154 students and 8 faculty. Of the students, 37 percent were women, far ahead of the Betty Coed movement of sixty years later. The school had been seventeen years in coming because of financial problems and the Civil War.

Folwell was dedicated to the university and to the cause of education. He laid the foundations and contributed mightily to both.

Dr. Martha Ripley

At age thirty-seven and after having three children, Martha Ripley went to medical school and graduated just as her husband became disabled. She specialized in children's diseases and obstetrics and founded the Maternity Hospital in St. Paul which, ahead of its time, accepted all patients, married or unmarried.

Ole Edvart Rolvaag

The author of *Giants of the Earth* emigrated to Minnesota from Norway and became a professor of Norwegian at St. Olaf College in Northfield. He did considerable writing but always in Norwegian so that his novels were necessarily first published in Norway and later translated into English. *Giants in the Earth* described the problems of an immigrant facing a change of culture such as so many Scandinavians did when they came to Minnesota to face a new language and a new culture and a very new country.

Rolvaag's son Karl became governor of Minnesota.

Roy Wilkins

Director of the NAACP from 1955 to 1977, responsible for much of the judicial successes of the Civil Rights Movement, winner of the coveted Springarn Medal and the United States Medal of Freedom, Roy Wilkins, though born in Chicago, was raised in St. Paul and graduated from the University of Minnesota. His activism was born when three black men were lynched in Duluth.

Frederick McGhee

His parents had been slaves in Mississippi. He opened a law practice in St. Paul in 1889, the first Afro-American criminal lawyer to practice in Minnesota and the first to practice west of the Mississippi.

In 1905 he formed the Niagara Movement, which was the predecessor of the NAACP. He made for himself and his family a place in this land of opportunity and set a pace for the Twin Cities to be in the forefront of civil rights. Possibly without his impetus, Hubert Humphrey would never have given the glorious keynote speech demanding civil rights at the 1948 Democratic National Convention.

Whitney Young

When Whitney Young came to the University of Minnesota for his graduate studies, the political climate encouraged him to become involved in the affairs of the National Urban League. He went on to become its executive director.

Dred Scott—Eliza Winton

Dred Scott was a black slave. In 1836 he was brought to Minnesota, always a free state, to serve his master, Dr. John Emerson, an army physician, when he was assigned to Fort Snelling. Mr. Scott married in Minnesota and had a child. When Dr. Emerson died, Mr. Scott became the property of the doctor's widow, who forced him to return to Missouri with her. The abolitionists helped him sue for his freedom on the basis that having once lived in a free territory he was no longer a slave. His case worked its way to the United States Supreme Court which ruled in 1857 that, while he may have been free in Minnesota, when he returned to the slave state of Missouri, his slave status was reattached.

In 1860 Colonel Christmas brought his slave Eliza Winton with him when he came from Memphis to vacation on the shores of Lake Harriet in Minneapolis' Chain of Lakes*. She was the widow of a free black. With the help of local abolitionists, the local court ruled that Ms. Winton was free. The Colonel gave no argument. The abolitionists paraded her around to show their victory. But the local resort and hotel owners were not happy with the effect the decision might have on their vacation business so they forced her to move to Canada. The abolitionists gave her nothing to help her along. Colonel Christmas gave her some money.

Pierre Radisson

With his brother-in-law Medard Chouart, Sieur des Groseilliers, he explored the southern shore of Lake Superior, wintering with the Indians in 1659. He took a rich crop of furs back to Montreal to show the potential of the region but was arrested by the French for fur trading without a license. He became so angry that he went to England and persuaded the English to explore the country and eventually to set up the Hudson Bay Company. This company

---

*   See Index or Contents for separate article on this topic.

became a major commercial factor in the area and still is throughout Canada.

A resort hotel was built on Christmas Lake at the turn of the century. The lake is just south of Lake Minnetonka and next to Lotus Lake, reputedly one of the only three places in America where lotus flowers grow naturally. The resort was named for Pierre Radisson. Eventually another Radisson Hotel was built in downtown Minneapolis. In the 1950s it was purchased by Curtis Carlson, an outstanding local entrepreneur with the Midas touch, who made it the anchor for an international hotel chain. The Inn on Christmas Lake burned down in the 1930s; the site was platted into homesites.

Joseph Nicolas Nicollet

A French astronomer and geographer arrived at Ft. Snelling in 1836 and was commissioned to map the area between the Mississippi and Missouri rivers. The result was some excellent and beautiful maps of Minnesota that became the standard for decades. A county and the main commercial street in Minneapolis were named for him. Another Nicollet, Jean, had discovered Lake Michigan two centuries earlier.

Nils Nyberg

In 1851 Nils Nyberg came to the Twin Cities Metropolitan Area, the very first Swede! He was different from other Minnesotans because of his light hair and fair coloring, so they called him the "foreigner." Fifteen years later, with the Civil War over and extensive marketing in Scandinavia, the Swedes and Norwegians and Danes flooded into the area and became its backbone.

Patty Berg

For nearly thirty years, from 1935 to 1964, Patty Berg dominated women's golfing in America, her red hair and freckles becoming a friendly and easily recognized symbol. She grew up in south Minneapolis and attended John Burroughs School just south of Lake Harriet when it was only a couple of portable buildings on the edge of town.

CHAPTER 10

Facts and Figures

Climate

Minnesotans love it! Many of them go north in the summer because it's too warm. The Chamber of Commerce says it's "brisk" in the dead of winter. People complain about the snow not coming soon enough or often enough. After all, in what other major metropolitan area can you go cross-country skiing out of your back door? Where else can you flood your backyard to make a hockey rink for the kids? Where else do people keep snowmobiles in their garages the way Arizonans keep golf carts? How many people know the joys of ice fishing, of sitting in a warm, cozy, little house on the middle of a lake where you can actually watch the fish nudge the bait through a hole in the ice, your car parked outside the door, or you can watch a football game on TV if the fish are slow?

Minnesotans love it. They design their houses, their clothes, their cars, their offices, shopping centers, and commercial areas to cope with it. Where else in the dead of winter can you get in your warm car in the warm garage attached to your warm house, drive downtown in your shirtsleeves to a warm parking ramp, and walk through the warm skyways to a warm office?

Major league games are played regardless of the weather. The Superbowl was played in Minneapolis in January, the day after a blizzard, in the Hubert Humphrey* Metrodome where the 50,000 fans sat in their shirtsleeves. The Twins haven't been rained out in years; they play in the Metrodome. You can watch the Vikings play NFL football in the Metrodome in your shirtsleeves regardless of the weather. The University of Minnesota's Big Ten football and baseball Golden Gophers play there. So do the state high school football playoffs. The Timberwolves play NBA basketball in the skyway-connected Target Center*, which is a venue for NHL hockey. It also houses, whatever the weather, circuses without tents and rock concerts without Woodstock's mud.

And in the Southern climes much vaunted for their winter warmth, where can the ladies bedeck themselves in full-length mink and little girls carry fancy fur hand warmers? You'd feel silly wearing a fur hat with earflaps in the South. There's a special feel and aroma to a pair of leather gloves. And there's a special elixir in crisp, cold air.

There are blizzards, two or three a year, mostly in November and March as the seasons change. But there is ample warning and no harm is ever done except maybe around the house by the kids who have to stay home from school. There are tornados in the early summer and fall. Occasionally a barn is blown down or a mobile home blown over, but nothing like the destruction of the earthquakes, or the forest fires, or the landslides, or the floods, or the hurricanes that blast much of the rest of the world.

Minnesota calls itself "The Theater of Seasons." There are some who say there are only two seasons: wintertime and highway construction time. But they're the skeptics.

---

*   See Index or Contents for separate article on this topic.

Winter is crisp and bright and has all its own sports and activities. Spring, after a hard winter, is the time for re-awakening, when the whites and grays and blacks turn green and pink. Summer fills the whole outdoors and the people swarm outside to enjoy it and eat bushels of Minnesota Golden Bantam corn on the cob, the best corn there is; not much is allowed to be shipped outside the state. Fall brings a feast of colors as the leaves change to their brilliant yellows and reds and browns in swirling patterns across the countryside, and the ducks and geese form up in their vees across the skies, and the apples are firm and sweet as they're plucked fresh from the trees, and you can see your breath a little as you watch the high school football teams ram their way up and down the white-striped field.

Population and Growth

Year	State	Anoka	Carver	Dakota	Hennepin	Ramsey	Scott	Washington	Total Metro
1850	6,077	-	-		584	-		2,227	-
1860	172,023	2,106	5,306	9,093	12,849	12,150	4,595	6,123	52,222
1870	439,706	3,940	11,586	16,312	31,566	23,085	11,042	11,809	109,340
1880	780,773	7,108	14,140	17,391	67,013	45,890	13,516	19,563	184,641
1890	1,301,283	9,884	16,534	20,240	185,294	39,796	13,831	25,992	311,571
1900	1,751,344	11,313	17,594	21,753	228,340	170,554	15,147	27,868	492,329
1910	2,075,908	12,493	17,155	21,733	333,480	223,675	14,888	26,013	649,437
1920	2,387,125	15,626	16,946	28,967	415,419	244,554	14,245	23,761	759,428
1930	2,583,953	18,415	16,936	34,592	517,785	286,721	14,116	24,753	913,318
1940	2,792,300	22,443	17,606	39,660	528,899	309,935	15,585	26,430	960,559
1950	2,982,483	35,579	18,155	49,019	676,579	355,332	16,486	21,909	1,173,059
1960	3,413,864	85,916	21,358	78,303	842,854	422,525	34,544	52,432	1,537,932
1970	3,805,000	154,712	28,331	139,808	960,080	476,784	32,433	83,003	1,875,131
1980	4,075,970	195,198	37,046	194,279	941,011	459,784	43,784	113,571	1,984,673
1990	4,375,099	243,644	47,915	275,227	1,032,431	485,765	57,846	145,896	2,288,724

The Larger Businesses

	[000,000]	Industrial	Service	Business
Alliant Techsystems	$1,187	#357	-	Defense equipment
Bemis	1,204	#323	-	Packaging, coatings
Best Buy	1,620	-	-	Consumer electronics
Cargill	46,500	-	-	Agricultural products
Carlson Companies	2,100	-	-	Travel, hotels, restaurants
Cenex	1,779	-	-	Agricultural coop
Ceridian	1,210	-	-	Data, employee services
Cray Research	895	#382	-	Large computers
C.H. Robinson	1,024	-	-	
Dayton-Hudson	10,778	-	#R-6	Retail merchandising
Deluxe Printers	1,582	#266	-	Business forms
Ecolabs	1,042	#361	-	Sanitary products
Fingerhut	1,606	-	-	Direct mail retail
First Bank System	1,864	-	B-31	Banking
3 M	13,883	# 31	-	Plastic products
General Mills	8,135	# 63	-	Cereals, food products
Harvest Stores	3,481	-	-	Agricultural supplies
H. B. Fuller	975	#368	-	Adhesives, sealants
Holiday	1,600	-	-	Consumer products
Honeywell	5,963	# 89	-	Temperature controls
IDS Life	28,040	-	#L-15	Life insurance
International Multifoods	2,224	#208	-	Food products
Jostens	915	#376	-	Commemorative jewelry
Land O' Lakes	2,733	#176	-	Dairy products
Lutheran Brotherhood	1,892	-	-	Life insurance
Medtronics	1,382	#300	-	Medical electronics
Metropolitan Financial	7,006	-	#I-12	Savings banking
Minnesota Mutual Life	7,804	-	#L-43	Life insurance
Nash-Finch	2,515	-	-	Food distribution
Northwest Airlines	7,571	-	#T-6	Airline
NWNL	1,378	-	-	Life insurance
Norwest Corporation	50,782	-	#B-14	General banking
Northern States Power	5,588	-	#U-44	Utilities
Pentair	1,328	#301	-	Portable tools

	[000,000]	Industrial	Service	Business
St. Paul Companies	17,149	-	#F-25	Insurance
Twin City Federal	5,026	-	#I-16	Savings banking
Toro	684	#470	-	Lawn care, snow removal
United Health	1,778	-	-	Hospitals
Valspar	694	#451	-	Paints, varnishes

Points of Pride

Lead in High School Education—"A newly released U.S. Census survey shows that . . . in the Twin Cities area, 90 percent of residents 25 and older have at least high school diplomas, putting the region in the top group among large metropolitan areas in high school education rates. . . ." *Star Tribune*, July 23, 1994

Business Climate—In a recent survey of the fifty best places in the world to do business, Hong Kong came in first. The Twin Cities were listed but numbers were only given to the first place.

Health—A survey by the Morgan Quitno Corp., reported in Florida's *Fort Myers News-Press* on March 23, 1995, rated Minnesota as the sixth healthiest state; Florida ranked fiftieth.

Health Care—The University of Minnesota Academic Health Center is among the ten best of the hundred academic health centers in the United States. It has an annual budget of $750 million and includes a medical school, a hospital, a public health school, and ancillary services.

Cost of Living Lower—Of the twenty largest metropolitan areas, only three have a lower cost of living than Minneapolis. *The Universal Almanac - 1993.*

Best Beer—In a contest in Denver in October 1994, Grain Belt Beer was given the gold medal as America's best beer. Coors was second. Grain Belt has been brewed in the same brewery, Nordeast*, for over a century, except for a hiatus during Prohibition.

Financial Rating Highest—According to Standard & Poor's, Minneapolis and Charlotte, N.C., are the only two cities in the country with a AAA bond rating, the highest possible rating. As a consequence, the two cities pay out lower amounts for interest when they borrow money for capital improvements.

Open Heart Surgery—The first open heart surgery in the country was performed at the University of Minnesota.

Health Care Tops—"A national study comparing health care in 16 metropolitan areas put the Twin Cities area at the top." *Star-Tribune*, September 27, 1994

Bone Marrow Transplants—The first bone marrow transplant in the United States was done at the University of Minnesota.

Shoreline Longest—Minnesota has more miles of shoreline than California, Florida, and Hawaii combined, more than 90,000 around its 15,291 lakes, which comprise 7,762 square miles or about 9 percent of the state's area, according to the publication *Hurray! Minnesota.*

Poverty Less—In a study by the Northwestern National Life Insurance Company analyzing sixteen metropolitan areas in the United States, the Twin cities were found to have only 5.7 percent of its families in the poverty level, the lowest rate of the areas surveyed. *Star-Tribune*, September 27, 1994

---

*   See Index or Contents for separate article on this topic.

Births to Teenagers Less—In a study by the Northwestern National Life Insurance Company analyzing sixteen metropolitan areas in the United States, only 2.5 percent of births in the Twin Cities were to mothers seventeen or younger, the lowest rate of the areas included in the study. *Star-Tribune*, September 27, 1994

Health Better—In a study by the Northwestern National Life Insurance Company analyzing sixteen metropolitan areas in the United States, the Twin Cities were found to have only 5.2 percent of its population in poor health, the lowest of the areas studied. *Star-Tribune*, September 27, 1994

More Large Businesses—In a study by the Northwestern National Life Insurance Company analyzing sixteen metropolitan areas in the United States, it was found that there were more large businesses per capita than any of the other areas. *Star-Tribune*, September 27, 1994

Economically Solid States—"Minnesota's economy is well diversified, has staunchly withstood the recent recession, and is growing nicely. In short, it's like a healthy stock portfolio, according to a recent study by Dun & Bradstreet. . . . The Twin Cities metropolitan area, which has half the businesses and two of every three jobs in the state, functions as the heart of the regional economy. The metro has a manufacturing base that compares with that of Cleveland, as well as growing financial and health service industries. . . . The median net income of $40,000 for Twin Cities-area households rivals that of New York and Seattle. . . ." *Star Tribune*, May 12, 1994.

Golf Most—Minnesota has more golfers per capita than any other state, maybe because so many people have been cooped up by a long winter, according to *Hurray! Minnesota*.

Green Index #5—In 1991 Minnesota ranked fifth out of the fifty states on an environmental green index done by the Institute for Southern Studies in Durham, N.C. Minnesota ranked behind Oregon, Maine, Vermont, and California. Minnesota was specifically praised for community health programs, groundwater protection efforts, and its "super-fund" for toxic waste cleanup, according to *Hurray! Minnesota*.

The Healthiest State—The *Health Care State Rankings 1994* rated Minnesota as the healthiest state in which to live ... [according to] Scott Morgan, president of Morgan Quitno, the Lawrence based publisher of state statistics.... "The second-annual rankings are based on twenty-three statistical factors of health, including the percentage of adults who smoke or are overweight, the death rate by AIDS and the percentage of drivers who wear seat belts. Positive factors include the number of community hospitals and the percentage of children entering kindergarten who are fully immunized. For example, Minnesota ranked forty-eighth in the number of births to teenage mothers...."

Crime Rate Low—The Twin Cities were second best of the twelve metro areas having between two and three million population. Of the metro areas having a similar crime rate, the Twin Cities have by far the largest [population, 20 percent larger than the other eleven cities combined]. *Star Tribune*, April 17, 1994

Death Rate Low—The Minneapolis death rate is lower than average. *Star Tribune*, May 15, 1994

Real Estate Values and Income High—In 1988 the property in downtown Minneapolis was worth $1.2 billion per square mile, plus that of St. Paul at $800 million. The greater metro area, twenty-three counties stretching from Rochester to St. Cloud, contains 1.2 percent of the nation's population but 1.3 percent of its personal income and 1.4 percent of its real property assets. *EURA Reporter*, Vol XXIV, No. 1, March 1994

National Sports Center—In one year, 1992, the Twin Cities were host to football's Superbowl, baseball's World Series, basketball's Final Four, and the U.S. Special Olympics.

Quality of Life—Every year or so around the country, studies are released as to the quality of life, measuring all manner of demographic criteria. The Twin Cities are almost always in the top, somewhere near Santa Barbara, frequently in first or second.

Growth Is High—Most surveys of such things in the past five years have found the Twin Cities to be the fastest growing metro area in the northern states between the Atlantic and the Rockies. *The Universal Almanac - 1993*

Unemployment Low—Minneapolis has the second lowest unemployment rate of any of the largest metropolitan areas. *The Universal Almanac - 1993*

Desirable Place to Live—"Despite its arctic winters, Minneapolis is one of the most desirable cities in the United States." *The Universal Almanac - 1993*

Skyway Systems

Minneapolis Skyways

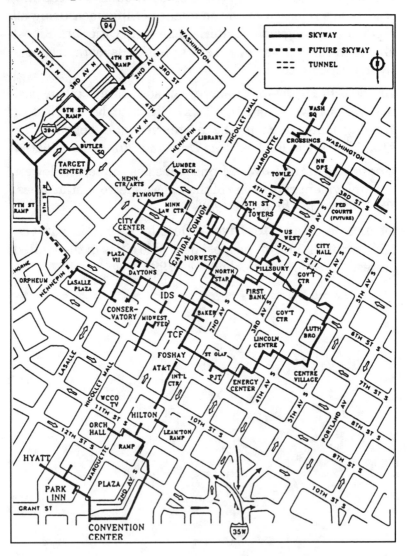

St. Paul Skyways

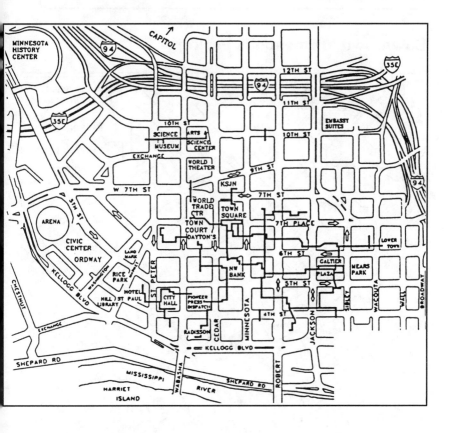

Parking Places

Downtown Minneapolis Parking

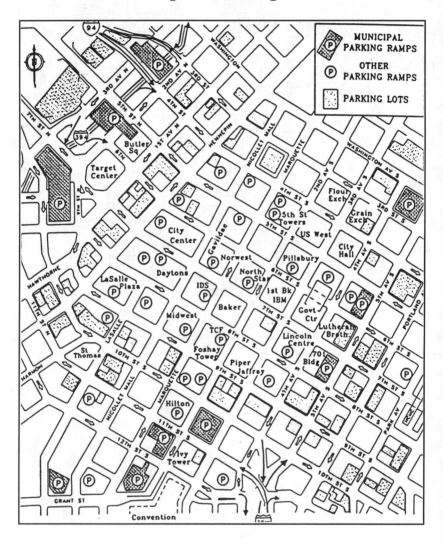

St. Paul Parking

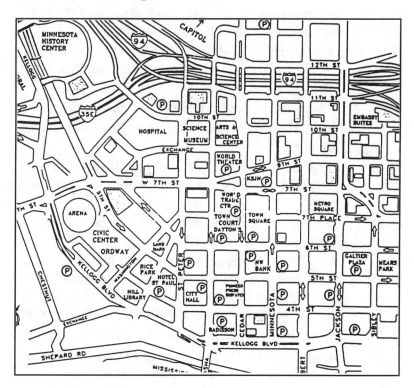

Trivia

Q-01   There was fierce competition to be the largest city in the state in the 1890 Census. Which city padded its figures, Minneapolis or St. Paul?

Q-02   In 1839 a duel was fought between James Thompson and Edward Phalen. What was the cause of the duel?

Q-03   Where was the world's first modern enclosed shopping mall located?

Q-04   When was the Nicollet Mall completed?

Q-05   For whom was Lake Harriet named?

Q-06   In what year did Zebulon Pike explore to the junction of the Minnesota and Mississippi rivers?

Q-07   How much did Zebulon Pike pay the Indians for the land at the confluence of the Minnesota and Mississippi rivers?

Q-08   What was the first name of Fort Snelling?

Q-09   What United States President commanded Fort Snelling?

Q-10   Large numbers of deer run wild throughout the Twin Cities. How many are killed by cars each year?

Q-11   On October 4, 1869, what major catastrophe did Minneapolis almost suffer?

Q-12   For years, campers have been spellbound by the nighttime cry of loons, which are the state bird. Loons prefer to nest each in a separate lake. Are there enough loons to populate Minnesota's lakes?

Q-13   When did St. Paul have its first Winter Carnival?

Q-14   When did John Dillinger, the most vicious criminal of the Depression Era, live in St. Paul?

Q-15   Hennepin and Ramsey counties have always been highly competitive. Which one held the first county fair?

Q-16   Which Historical House was pulled from its original location to its present location by relays of children?

Q-17   Snow and ice make the streets and highways slippery in the winter. A mixture of salt and sand is used to combat it. How much salt does Hennepin County use in an average winter?

Q-18   When the first settlers came in the 1850s, what was the cost of land?

Q-19   Does snow have any redeeming qualities besides being beautiful and slippery under skis?

Q-20   How did the ancient rivalries of the Ojibwas and the Dakotas find a resolution in modern times?

Q-21   When and where was the first Russian Orthodox Church built in the Lower 48?

Q-22   Henry Wadsworth Longfellow wrote a long and engaging poem about Gitche-Gumee, Nokomis, Hiawatha, and Minnehaha, "The Song of Hiawatha," but he was never in Minnesota. How did he find his inspiration?

Q-23   The Mendota Bridge crosses the Mississippi at Fort Snelling. What is unique about the bridge?

Q-24   When did school start in Minnesota?

◆ ◆ ◆

A-01   Civic pride triumphed over virtue in both cities; St. Paul added 9,000, Minneapolis added 18,000.

A-02   Phalen stole Thompson's pet pig. Thompson won, nicking Phalen. A lake was named for Phalen in St. Paul.

A-03   Southdale in Edina, built in 1956 with Dayton's, Donaldson's, Sears, and Penney's as anchors. The basic concept was so logical that it was copied around the country and around the world. It is a wonderland for shoppers and the devil incarnate for smaller merchants, though these have survived well by catering to their immediate locales.

A-04   In 1967, just in time to be featured on an early "Mary Tyler Moore Show." It was totally updated in 1992. It is a miracle mile of shops and stores, of sidewalk cafes and a Hmong farmers market on summer Thursdays, of water statuary, a delightful park with falls and a pond next to Orchestra Hall, and the entrance to the Loring Greenway that leads amid flowers and trees and teeter-totters over to Loring Park and the Statuary Park beside it.

A-05 Harriet Leavenworth, the wife of the colonel who initiated construction of Fort Snelling. A well-known federal prison is located in a city in Kansas named for her husband.

A-06 1805, he had not peaked yet.

A-07 Sixty gallons of whisky and $200 worth of trinkets. It's worth billions now because of the development that followed its opening to Europeans.

A-08 Fort St. Anthony was built in 1821 and expanded and renamed in 1835. As the Mississippi was the life-stream of the Twin Cities, Fort Snelling was the originating hub.

A-09 Zachary Taylor was commandant from 1828 to 1829.

A-10 About 3,000, causing close to $2 million in damages to the cars plus large bursts of anger when they eat thousands of backyard gardens just as they come ripe. Since firearms cannot be discharged inside the metropolitan area, the deer lead a charmed life and multiply with great abandon. Currently bows and arrows are being used as a small control. The Canadian geese, a rarity thirty years ago, now dwell in the thousands in parks and golf courses, cleverly leaving their droppings in the places most used by humans. Hundreds are taken to Oklahoma every year, but reproduction quickly replaces them.

A-11 A tunnel dug under St. Anthony Falls collapsed on October 4, 1869, threatening to destroy the falls. An emergency was declared and all able-bodied citizens were required to help fill in the tunnel, which they did in time. Had they failed, the saw-mills and flour mills upon which Minneapolis wholly depended would have been lost. It cost a million dollars for the filling and shoring of the falls, possibly equivalent to a hundred million dollars today. Little is said today of who dug the tunnel and who gave him permission, if anyone.

A-12   There are 15,291 lakes of five or more acres. There are only 12,000 loons and, like people, they prefer to nest in pairs. It's possible that you have to be a Minnesotan to appreciate the loon.

A-13   The first St. Paul Winter Carnival was opened on February 1, 1886, to prove that large-scale fun things can happen in the winter. The first Ice Palace was 140 feet long and 106 feet high. It required 200 men and $5,210 to build. The 1992 ice palace was 150 feet high with nine towers capping its crenallated walls. The palaces, constructed with much fanfare most every year, are made of thousands of large blocks of ice hauled in from Lake Como and then lighted with floodlights of changing colors. Large and intricate ice sculptures are built for the Carnival in Rice Park, over by the Ordway*. Ice fishing contests are held in the parks, and if the snow pack is adequate, a sled dog race may come down from Duluth.

A-14   In 1934. According to a wide belief, for a time during the Depression, many criminals were permitted to live in St. Paul as long as they committed no crimes there and prevented others from engaging in criminal activity, making St. Paul a peaceful city until the privilege was abused.

A-15   Hennepin held its county fair in 1855, three years before Minnesota was even a state. The first State Fair was in 1859, Minnesota's second year as a

---

*   See Index or Contents for separate article on this topic.

state. Afterwards, state fairs have always been held in Ramsey County, though very close to the Hennepin line. About a million and a half people usually attend.

A-16   The Stevens House* built in 1849. Mary Stevens, the first white child born in Minnesota, lived there. In the 1920s teams of school children tugged it to its present location in Minnehaha Park.

A-17   During the 1988-89 winter, Hennepin County used 18,000 *tons* of salt, give or take a few pounds. Of course Ramsey and the other metropolitan counties plus the state, the cities, and the towns used four or five times that amount. Every winter there is a debate: Should we continue to use salt which damages the environment and rusts out car bodies, or should we stop using salt and accept the slip-and-fall personal injuries and fender-bender accidents as part of the turf? There are obviously varied protagonists for both points of view.

A-18   If the land was homesteaded, it cost $1.25 an acre, but the homesteader had to occupy and cultivate it for five years. Non-homestead land went for $8.50 an acre, both of them such a bargain that waves of Scandinavians and Germans swarmed to the land, providing Minnesota with a stability and populism which have served it well. Besides the attraction of the price, they found that the gently rolling land of lakes and forests reminded them of their homeland and that it was among the most fertile land in the world.

A-19   Layers of snow insulate the ground against more intense cold, and the snow absorbs nitrates, cal-

---

*   See Index or Contents for separate article on this topic.

cium, potassium, and sulfates from the air and releases them into the ground. And it makes spring even more wonderful.

A-20 They were urged in 1968 to speak with a common voice on civic affairs and civil rights. Three of them, Dennis Banks, Clyde Bellecourt, and Russell Means, met at length and formed A.I.M., the American Indian Movement, which moved into national prominence as a voice of Native Americans. Clyde later became best man at Dennis' wedding. Peggy Bellecourt became an effective protest leader.

A-21 In Nordeast Minneapolis in 1888 to serve the growing group of immigrants from Russia. The Russian Orthodox Church is now increasingly serving the new wave of immigrants from the former Soviet Union who are settling in the Twin Cities. Russian is one of the numerous languages heard when strolling along the Nicollet Mall.

A-22 Alex Hessler made a daguerreotype of Minnehaha Falls which he gave to a friend who showed it to Longfellow. The rest is poetry. There is a statue of Hiawatha carrying Minnehaha across the stream just above the falls, which is a beautiful, curved cascade just before the confluence of Minnehaha Creek with the Mississippi River. About a mile farther upstream, the creek flows through Lake Nokomis. Gitche-Gumee, Longfellow's name for Lake Superior, is a proudful place for Minnesotans. A magnificent drive is the 150 miles from Duluth along the "North Shore" to Thunder Bay in Canada. The shoreline is mostly rockbound, wild, and heavily forested, awesome when the great waves come in during a storm from this largest lake in the world. The lake on the north side is seldom warm enough for swimming.

A-23   The bridge across the deep valley of the Mississippi and the mouth of the Minnesota is 4,119 feet
long, .8 miles. When it was built in 1924-1926 it
was the longest continuous concrete arch span in
the world. In 1992-1994 it was totally rebuilt from
the arches up, widening it from its four lanes and
adding complicated interchanges at both ends to
accommodate the great increase of traffic generated by the Lindberg International Airport (the
twenty-first busiest in the world) and the residential growth spreading the metropolitan area
towards Rochester to the southeast.

A-24   In 1823 inside the protective walls of Fort
Snelling. The first hospital, the first church, and
the first circulating library were also organized
there.

Statistics

METRO

Airports

International Airport	1
Arrivals & departures [1993]	439,990
Passengers annually [1993]	23,402,412
Reliever Airports	6

Bus Transportation (Metropolitan Transit Commission)

Passengers	66,510,000
Mile	30,040,122
Buses	970
Lift equipped	161
Vehicles for disabled	232
Disabled passengers	1,136,504

Colleges & Universities
(4 year liberal arts) 11

Media
Radio stations 30
Television stations 7
Newspapers (daily) 2

Sports Attendance
(Major professional leagues)
Timberwolves 754,593
Twins 2,048,673
Vikings 539,015

MINNEAPOLIS

Arts & Cultural Organizations
Theaters 28
Art Galleries 101
Dance Groups 8
Feature Films shot in last 10 years 21

Budget (1994 estimate) $696,000,000

Buildings
Building permits issued 9,085
Tallest buildings
    IDS Center (57 stories) . . . . 775'
    First Bank Place (55 stories) . . . . . . 775'
    Norwest Center (57 stories) . . . . . . 773'

City Employees (non-school) 5,877

Conventions
Events 225
Delegates 213,780

Fire Department
Fire alarms 9,439
Medical emergencies 20,555

Sworn personnel   431
Civilian Personnel   20
Fire trucks   32

Geography
Latitude . . . . N 44° 58' 39"
Longitude . . . . W 93° 15' 56"
Altitude . . . .   834'
Area . . . . square miles 58.7, acres 37,244
Land acres 35,244
Water acres 2,324
Lakes   17

Hospitals   7

Hotels
Number   15
Rooms 5,000

Housing
Family Households 77,671
Non-family Households 83,011
Units 176,563
Price, median for all homes $75,900
Rent, average for 2 or more bedrooms . . . $552

Jobs & Income
Labor force (civilian) 206,289
Unemployment (November 1992) 4.8%
Median household income $25,324
Per capita income $14,830

Library
Facilities   16
Collections 3,070,698
Loaned items 3,226,596
Registered borrowers 435,692

Office Buildings (downtown)

Buildings 79
Space . . . . 20,982,119'

Parks (city only)

Number 170
Total acres 6,385
Recreation centers in parks 44
Swimming beaches 11
Swimming pools 11
Golf courses 8
Tennis courts 192
Hiking trail miles 39
Biking trail miles 38
Ice rinks - indoor 9
Ice rinks - outdoor 85

Parking Spaces 57,000

Police

Sworn personnel 848
Civilian personnel 174
Police dogs 14
Calls for service 362,512

Population

White (78%) 288.967
Black (13%) 47,948
American Indian (3%) 12,335
Asian (4%) 15,723
Other (1%) 3,410

Minneapolis Population History

1860..........	2,564	1930..........	464,356
1870..........	13,066	1940..........	492,370
1880..........	46,887	1950..........	521,718
1890..........	164,738	1960..........	482,872
1900..........	202,718	1970..........	434,400
1910..........	301,408	1980..........	371,000
1920..........	380,582	1990..........	368,383

Recycling & Waste
Dwelling units serviced   116,000
Household garbage, tons   104,700
Newspapers, cans, glass, etc. recycled, tons .   22,000
Yard waste recycled, tons   16,700
Large metals & appliances recycled, tons . .   2,250

Schools
Public . .   Elementary 60, Secondary 22, Pupils 43,932
Private . . Elementary and Secondary 35, Pupils 6,517
Employees (public schools)   6,000

Minneapolis Skyways 1994   62
Blocks connected by skyways   49
Miles of skyways   5

Minneapolis Streets & Blocks
Street miles   1,078
Alley miles   445
Block size, average . . . . 330' x 660'
Blocks, number   6,000
Bridges   571

Vital Statistics
Births   6,273
Deaths   3,577

Water and Sewers
Water consumption (gallons) 22,012,000
Utility holes   55,000

Weather
Rain and snow . . . .   32.21"
Snow . . . .   47.40"
Average temperatures
    January . . . .   15°
    April . . . .   44°
    July . . . .   70°
    October . . . .   47°

What's in a Name

Bloomington   Named by the first settlers who arrived in 1852 after the city of Bloomington, Illinois

Burnsville   Named by the Burns family when they moved to the Twin Cities area from Canada

Duluth   Daniel Greysolon, Sieur du Lhut, a French explorer who canoed across Lake Superior to what is now the city of Duluth and then explored farther into central Minnesota

Edina   A contraction of Edinburgh in Scotland, itself apparently signifying Eden City, or city of paradise

Hennepin   A French explorer-priest, the first European to see the Falls of St. Anthony, the only falls on the Mississippi

Hopkins   A second tier suburb of Minneapolis, named by its first postmaster for himself

Itasca   The "True Head" (Latin: verITAS CAput), a name coined by Henry Schoolcraft when he found the head of the Mississippi in Lake Itasca in northwestern Minnesota

Lafayette   A bay in Lake Minnetonka named for the Marquis de Lafayette, a Frenchman who provided great help to the Americans during their Revolution

LaSalle   A French explorer of the Mississippi who sent Father Hennepin north to the St. Anthony Falls

Le Sueur
A French fur trader based at Fort Snelling who explored up the Minnesota River as far as present day Mankato

Marquette
A French priest who in 1673 explored from Machimillimac in Michigan westward into Minnesota. He is the only priest-explorer still often spoken of as "Pere Marquette" rather than "Father Marquette."

Minneapolis
A combination of the Dakota word *minne* for water and the Greek suffix *polis* for city, a name for "The City of Lakes"

Minnehaha
A combination of the Dakota words *minne* for water and *haha* for laughing

Minnetonka
A named coined by Alexander Ramsey from the Dakota words *minne* for water and *tonka* for big

Mound
The city is named after Indian burial mounds in the neighborhood. There once were hundreds of such mounds scattered around the state. Some mounds located west of Lake Calhoun were the cause of much speculation; one view strongly held by some insisted that they were burial mounds of one of the ten Lost Tribes of Israel; another view insisted equally strongly that they were of a Mongolian tribe.

New Brighton
A first tier suburb of Minneapolis named for Brighton in Massachusetts

Nicollet
A French fur trader who explored the southern areas of Minnesota

Ojibwe
We meaning "to roast" and *ojib* meaning "to pucker," usually translated as "to roast until puckered"

Osseo   Named for one of the characters de-
                         scribed in Longfellow's "Song of
                         Hiawatha"

Pig's Eye   Louis Parrant* whose eye seemed to
                         some to resemble a pig's eye, set up a bar
                         in a cave on the Mississippi where St.
                         Paul now stands. The bar drew substan-
                         tial crowds for the time and became so
                         well known that a letter could be ad-
                         dressed simply to "Pig's Eye" and it
                         would be delivered. A priest, father Gau-
                         tier, built a chapel dedicated to St. Paul
                         and persuaded the town fathers that St.
                         Paul would be a better name for the ages
                         than Pig's Eye.

Radisson   A French fur trader who explored into
                         Minnesota. His true name was Pierre
                         Esprit.

St. Anthony   The patron saint of Father Hennepin
                         who gave its name to the only falls on the
                         Mississippi. The Dakotas knew the falls
                         as *Minnerara*, curling water, or as *Owah
                         Menah*, falling waters.

St. Louis Park   A first tier suburb of Minneapolis named
                         for the Minneapolis & St. Louis Rail-
                         road, the Twin Cities' first railroad
                         south

White Bear   The name given because Indians in the
Lake   area believed that the spirit of a sacred
                         white bear lived in the lake

---

*   See Index or Contents for separate article on this topic.

Minnesota State Emblems

State Tree: Norway Pine
State Bird: Loon
State Fish: Walleye
State Flower: Pink & White Ladyslippper
State Gemstone: Lake Superior Agate
State Grain: Wild Rice
State Mushroom: Morrel

Index

Other Books From Republic of Texas Press

Call Wordware Publishing, Inc. for names of the bookstores in your area: (214) 423-0090

To The Tyrants Never Yield: A
Texas Civil War Sampler
by Kevin R. Young

Tragedy at Taos: The Revolt
of 1847
by James A. Crutchfield

A Trail Rider's Guide to Texas
by Mary Elizabeth Sue Goldman

Unsolved Texas Mysteries
by Wallace O. Chariton

Western Horse Tales
Edited by Don Worcester

Wild Camp Tales
by Mike Blakely

Seaside Press

The Bible for Busy People
Book 1: The Old Testament
by Mark Berrier Sr.

Critter Chronicles
by Jim Dunlap

Dallas Uncovered
by Larenda Lyles Roberts

Dirty Dining: A Cookbook,
and More, for Lovers
by Ginnie Siena Bivona

Exotic Pets: A Veterinary
Guide for Owners
by Shawn Messonnier, D.V.M.

I Never Wanted to Set the
World on Fire, but Now That
I'm 50, Maybe It's a Good Idea
by Bob Basso, Ph.D.

Just Passing Through
by Beth Beggs

Kingmakers
by John R. Knaggs

Lives and Works of the
Apostles
by Russell A. Stultz

Los Angeles Uncovered
by Frank Thompson

Only: The Last Dinosaur
by Jim Dunlap

Seattle Uncovered
by JoAnn Roe

San Antonio Uncovered
by Mark Louis Rybczyk

A Sure Reward
by B.J. Smagula

Survival Kit for Today's
Family
by Bill Swetmon

They Don't Have to Die
by Jim Dunlap

Twin Cities Uncovered
by The Arthurs

Your Puppy's First Year
by Shawn Messonnier, D.V.M.

Call Wordware Publishing, Inc. for names of the
bookstores in your area: (214) 423-0090